Managing Performance at Work

A Step-by-Step Guide

MG, you are my rock.

About this Workbook

'People are our greatest asset' has become a cliché through over-use, though it is clearly true for many organisations, and is usually a reflection of the quality of the management and leadership they experience at work. People usually are our greatest operating expense, however, and well managed people will definitely help an organisation to grow. Managing performance - especially poor performance - is an issue facing almost every single organisation. Some managers mistakenly view performance management as a task to be carried out by HR professionals. Others feel uncomfortable having difficult conversations, and don't want to damage relationships with the people in their teams. Other managers set ambiguous objectives, then struggle to understand if performance targets have truly been met. Occasionally, a manager will claim that they shouldn't need to follow the prescribed company process, because any good manager will set targets anyway; sounds good in principle, but then they don't follow the process OR set targets, which means that the managers are part of the problem, and should be subject to prompt improvement planning themselves.

You might think that a formal performance management process is only for large organisations, but even the largest organisations started out small once upon a time, and they grew because they had good people working at the right level. This applies then to organisations of any size, because it's all about creating a culture of success.

The book, the advice and guidance, and the activities and checklists within are all based on real organisational experience, gathered in the course of managing real people in real businesses. Rooted in business psychology and management best practice, there will be plenty of real and workable solutions to help you navigate the great responsibility of managing others, and to create a high-performance culture, polishing your reputation as an inspirational manager and leader of people.

We also offer company-wide training workshops, tailored for new managers and experienced managers alike, designed to ensure that all managers fully understand their performance management obligations, and work together consistently to build clear expectations, a strong ethos of business improvement and a high-performance culture. Check out our website www.catapultconsulting.co.uk to read about the work we do and some of our clients, and discover the many ways in which we can help you.

Contact us via our website if you would like to discuss personalising this workbook for your organisation, adding your branding, your process and your language for the perfect cultural fit for your business.

Why You Should Read This Book

There are many books available on the subject already, so how is this one different? This workbook serves as a standalone self-directed learning activity. New managers can read through the chapters, complete the exercises and develop their confidence and competence in the art of managing high performance. Time-served managers can use it to review their practices, and see how they might update the way they work with others.   HR professionals might give a copy to new starters to set some clear expectations, and ensure a level playing field or choose to use the text as a workbook to accompany in-house courses.

Some organisations do little or nothing to help new managers to understand what managing performance effectively means. You can sit and wait for some training, or you can work through this book, apply the tips and techniques, and become a first-class line manager without anyone's help.

At Catapult Consulting, we have over 30 years of experience of being managed, of being managers, of managing managers, of training, leading, coaching and consulting to build high performance. As well as working with public and private sector organisations all over the world, we also teach our practices and insights, tools and techniques at various UK universities, and receive great feedback for the plain language, the relevance to today's organisations, and the ease of application.

Introduction

Your organisation may enjoy state-of-the-art design facilities, world class manufacturing capabilities, leading edge technology, best practice policies and processes... but it is still your PEOPLE who actually do most of the work. Even organisations relying heavily on artificial intelligence know that their software is only as good as the people who designed it.

This workbook has been created to help you follow a logical sequence to manage the performance of people in your team, and to support the continuous development of a high-performance culture within your business. Suitable for office-based, hybrid or remote team working, spanning any industry, it will provide you with business tools, techniques and practical ideas to help you in your leadership practice, plus questions to get you thinking about how you can play your part in improving performance across your business.

Each section has been carefully designed to guide your thinking and provide advice on planning and preparation for conversations with team members, from setting targets to checking on progress, and when necessary, to have those difficult conversations about underperformance that we all dread. It will help you at every stage of managing an employee. We have also answered the most frequently asked questions (FAQ), based on our experience of running this program for many major organisations.

Good managers support every stage of the end-to-end employment process, and most of us can recall a really good manager who helped us to grow and develop our career. This is your chance to be that great manager who your people remember.

Ultimately, there is no substitute for practice, and your greatest learning will come from applying what you read here and discussing with your colleagues.

Managing people is one of the greatest privileges you will ever have in your professional life. This workbook is about how you can **contribute** to the growth and development of the people in your team.

Wherever you see this toolkit icon, this indicates that the model, checklist or structure is a highly relevant, immediately applicable and historically proven business tool to help you coach and manage your people to high performance. You can use the tools on a daily basis to raise your management game.

There are a lot of these toolkit icons throughout this book. That's because although the book is carefully rooted in academic theory, it is written to be immediately relatable, relevant, and practical, and to help you to be the very best manager you can be.

In fact, you can get started on putting them into practice right away!

Referenced throughout this workbook are some brilliant thinkers and theorists, and for a fuller understanding of their work, please take a look at the reading list at the back of the book.

Contents

Chapter One: The High-Performance Mindset

You, the Manager!

Why do you want to be a manager? Is it the money? The status? The power? The career advancement? Or is it because you're really passionate about helping people to grow? When we manage other people, we need to make sure that we are in the right mindset. A job in management may well pay more, but your work will shift from doing the job yourself, to getting it done through other people.

Different Career Trajectories

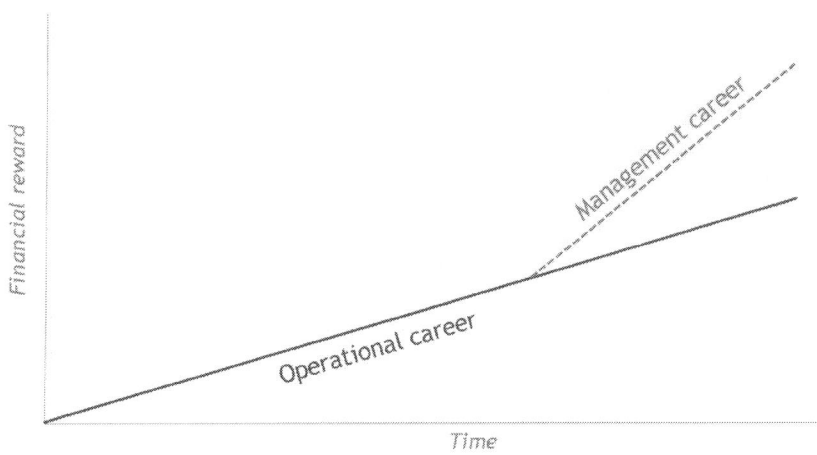

No doubt your salary will increase faster if you pursue a career in management (and ultimately, on into leadership), but are you really cut out for it? Many strong operational performers may be attracted to a career in management under the mistaken expectation that they will simply be doing more of the same kind of work, but at a higher level and for more money. What many aspiring managers don't consider is that management is all about people: setting goals, managing performance, communicating important business messages, scheduling the work, signing off sickness, absence, holidays, and managing conflict. These are rarely the same skills that got them noticed in the first place, and it is little wonder that star operational performers often make mediocre managers.

Arguably, 75% of a manager's job is communication, and regardless of how many channels of communication exist within your organisation, your team will look to their line manager to keep them informed about matters which affect them, and that includes providing honest and timely feedback about their performance. Ultimately, every element of a manager's job is about managing performance.

As manager, you can't be too nice, but you can be too weak. If you allow a poor performer to go unchallenged, the other members of your team will start to relax their efforts, and suddenly you may find that you have an entire team which is under-performing. Why should they work hard if one of their colleagues isn't putting in the hours? Don't fool yourself into thinking that the other team members won't notice... they most definitely will! And nothing demotivates a good employee like watching you tolerate a bad one.

You don't have to be a bully, either... nobody likes a bully! One grievance raised against you might be seen as a difference of personalities, but more than one will start to impact on your credibility and even on your own career potential.

You need to find the courage to give honest feedback in a timely way to each member of your team. That way, they are absolutely clear on what is expected of them, and can make informed career choices for themselves.

Employees don't usually come to work with the intention of doing a bad job, but sometimes they do get disengaged, and for a variety of reasons. The line manager's job is to help each employee to feel engaged at work.

Sometimes an employee may have gone several years without having a manager with the courage to challenge poor performance. This doesn't mean that it's too late for you to do it now. In fact, the employee will probably be quite relieved to have some honesty for once, and respect you for it. It's also an important part of the manager-employee relationship. Your team members are expecting it of you; it's what managers do.

Many managers tend to think that managing performance and having the difficult conversations should be the responsibility of the HR team, but that's not the case.

If that was HR's job, why would the company need you?

Did you know: Almost 80% of unfair dismissal claims which end up in employment tribunal are won by the employee. This doesn't mean the company was wrong to fire them. It almost always means that the manager simply didn't follow the company's own written performance management procedure. Check with HR to make sure you are following their rules, and keep your company out of court.

Let's be 100% clear about who does what in the performance management process, so that managing the performance of your people never falls between the cracks.

HR's Job:

- To design the performance management process
- To design and distribute the associated paperwork – hard/soft copy
- To keep a signed copy of the paperwork on file, verifying that an employee has received and understood it
- To provide training in performance management, where requested
- To agree with the leadership team the timings of the performance year: when to set goals, when to review goals, when (if) to do an interim appraisal, and when to give the final performance review
- To give advice and guidance if you need to pursue a formal disciplinary process on the grounds of conduct or performance
- Getting legal advice in the event of an employment tribunal

Your Job:

- Setting clear expectations about the role and level of performance required
- To manage people on a daily basis, regardless of when / where they work
- To set clear and compelling performance goals
- To measure progress against those goals
- To provide regular feedback on performance and behaviour
- To make recommendations for improvement and development
- To follow the process defined by HR
- To coach your people for growth

Many new managers (and far too many experienced managers) don't realise the extent of their responsibilities, and prefer to stay focused on operational tasks that are safely within their comfort zones. But that's not what management is about!

A company's performance management procedure (one of HR's responsibilities) usually outlines the exact process which a manager and employee <u>must</u> follow in the event of misconduct or poor performance. This procedure is supplied to the employee when they join the company, and forms part of their contract of employment.

Activity 1.1: Focus on Your Team

This workbook is a practical guide filled with activities and exercises you can do to create a high performance culture. Let's frame the rest of the workbook by making a list of all the people who directly report into you.

Person: Role:

Person: Role:

Person: Role:

Person: Role:

Person: Role:

Person: Role:

Person: Role:

Person: Role:

Remember to include contractors, interim or temporary / agency staff, because they are members of your team, and managing their performance is still your responsibility.

Person: Role:

Person: Role:

Motivation: The Key to High Performance

Motivation can be defined as the direction and intensity of effort has been the subject of academic research for over 100 years. When we can understand what really interests another person, we can work out how to get them to do what we want. This is crucial when driving the performance of individual team members at work. And let's not forget that performance management means managing and sustaining good performance, as well as challenging poor performance.

If you ask somebody why they go to work, they will probably mention all the usual extrinsic motivators (material rewards rooted in external perceptions of success) first:

- Salary, benefits, bonus, promotion, status, grade rise, winning, recognition, fear of failure.

But if you dig a little deeper, people often start to mention other things, the intrinsic motivators, (things that people care much more deeply):

- Social interaction, learning and growth, to apply their knowledge, to have fun, for self-expression, to fulfil a sense of purpose, and to make a difference.

Fact: Most people will claim that they come to work for the money. In fact, money is only part of the motive; it's much more about what money will enable a person to do. There is no doubt that the less money someone earns, the more important it will be to them. But research into high performing sports professionals has shown that players who are intrinsically motivated (to be the very best player they can be, to achieve their personal best, to contribute to a successful team, and to represent their team or country) generally outperform those players who are more interested in fees, bonuses and celebrity parties.

Occasionally, a manager will share a view that you have to shout at employees, and maybe even threaten them in order to get them to do what you want. Fear-based 'motivation' is actually intimidation, and will lead to poorer performance, and a heap of grievances raised against you.

FAQ: But most people are just interested in the money!

If an employee is only motivated by the financial reward, they will continue to work for you as long as they get paid, but they may also leave without hesitation if one of your competitors offers them more money. If someone is motivated by more than just money, they will still expect to get paid for their time, but will be more likely to go the extra mile, care about the long-term success of the team and organisation, and be much more loyal to their employer. Which type of employee would you rather have?

FAQ: Yeah, but I still think people are only interested in the money!

Research by Aviva insurance in 2021 identified that 1 in 4 people who retire early choose to go back to work, and for a number of intrinsic reasons, including boosting their mental wellbeing, wanting a new sense of purpose, and for the social interaction.

Let's look at it another way. Imagine that you have won the lottery – many, many millions – and are set for life, never needing to work another day as long as you live. How will you spend your time? Most people talk about travelling – a world cruise, enjoying the finest luxury money can buy. So how long will you travel... forever? Or maybe a year? And then what? People often say next that they would buy a big house in the country, with horses, and swimming pool. OK! So, what will you do with your day? Sit by the pool and drink champagne, they declare. Every day for a week? Yes! Every day for a month? Yes. Every day for a year? Well, no probably not... people start to get a bit bored after a while, and pleasure habituates, which means that what was exciting at the start becomes boring quite quickly. So, then what? That's when the conversations with our clients start getting **really** interesting! People talk about things such as founding a charity, or starting a social enterprise, or helping out with local schools or voluntary organisations. Why bother? Because it gives them a sense of purpose, a sense of meaning, and of making a difference. We all need money to pay our bills; that much is certain. But after a while, people look for greater meaning and a sense of making a difference. That becomes much more important to us in the long term, because it's how we are wired as human beings.

FAQ: But not everyone wants to progress!

Some high performing employees will simply want to come to work to do a good job, and then go home. They aren't interested in career advancement, or accessing training, and are perfectly happy working at the same level, doing the same thing day after day. As long as that performance meets the requirements of the role, then it is fine to support them in continuing to work in that way. But if the work changes, or the targets increase and that person starts to fall behind, that will eventually become a performance management issue which needs addressing.

Alternatives to Financial Reward

You may not have a big budget or be able to afford to pay your team members the amount they think they deserve. But you can consider other elements of motivation - such as personal and professional aspirations - and think about meeting some of those needs, instead. How can you give them more of what they really want? We will explore that later in activity 1.3.

For example, paying for a recognised qualification (HNC, NVQs, PRINCE2 or other professional qualification) will make them a more desirable employee, and give them greater employment security.

There is more on this topic in chapters 6 and 7.

FAQ: But what happens if you pay for training for your people, and then they leave anyway?

Ah, but what if you don't train them, and they stay?!

Activity 1.2: What Motivates YOU?

Let's start by thinking about what really motivates YOU to come to work, and do this job. You might just surprise yourself!

	Reason	Your Score ✓
A	Money (lifestyle, provide for family etc)	
B	To learn and grow	
C	For the social interaction	
D	To do interesting work	
E	To get out of the house	
F	Because daytime TV is rubbish!	
G	Working gives me a sense of achievement	
H	To set a good example to my kids	
I	To use my education and skills	
J	To get promoted	
K	To be a good citizen	
L	To make a difference	

In the table, there is a list of the common reasons people mention about why they come to work. Take a few minutes now to complete this activity. Compare each reason (starting with A) with each of the other reasons (B, C, D…L) and put a tick in the score column. So, when comparing reason A (money) with reason B (to learn and grow), if you feel that money is more important to you than learning and growth, simply put a tick in your score column against A. Then compare A (money) and C (social interaction). If social interaction is more important to you, put a tick against C, but if money is still more important, put another tick against A. Compare reason A with all the other following reasons in turn, working down the list. Then do the same with B, comparing with each of the other subsequent reasons. Note: You don't need to compare upwards (B or A) because you already did that when you were comparing reason A against all other criteria.   The last paired comparison will be K vs L.

Tip: Put a ✓ in the corresponding box each time you select one option over another. Add them up once you have compared each item with each of the others.

Well, was it what you first thought?

What were your top three?

-
-
-

People are not all motivated the same, and we do well not to make assumptions about them. When you can reward high performance with something that really matters to an employee, they will likely feel even more motivated.

Next, do this exercise with your team members to find out what really drives them. It may surprise you to see how diverse their motivators are.

Activity 1.3: SPACE Analysis

Strengths, Priorities, Aspirations, Competences, Experience

How well do you know your people?

This section will help team leaders and people managers to understand what drives the people they are managing. It can be used to help team members to align around a common goal or set of goals, or to create a team charter of expected behaviours and performance. It is invaluable when working to support individual career development and maintain a healthy work life balance. You can use this form to interview each member of your team. Interviews are more effective than just getting the other person to fill in the details themselves because it helps you really to understand things from their perspective.

But first, let's start with you!

Once you have answered these questions for yourself, it will be easier to understand the relevance of asking the same questions to your people.

Over the page, you will find some suggested questions for understanding motivation on a deeper level. Go through and answer them for yourself to build your self-awareness.

Experience shows that employees really enjoy the process of being asked about what's important to them. It makes them feel much more appreciated.

What are the consequences of NOT asking about strengths, priorities, aspirations, competences and experience?

_____

_____

_____

_____

STRENGTHS

Most people are very familiar with their weaknesses, having had them pointed out all through their lives! But get people talking about their strengths, and you get a powerful insight into what they do best, what they enjoy, and what makes them proud. This will help you to allocate the workload to the best people for the job.

- What are your strengths? What do you find straightforward, really easy and enjoyable to do?

- What are your particular areas of interest when you are reading books, journals or searching the net?

- Which strengths do you rely on when dealing with challenging situations?

- What are your key strengths when working with others?

- Which strengths do your colleagues admire you for?

- What feedback have you received in the past about your strengths?

PRIORITIES

Understanding an employee's personal situation will help you as manager not to put undue pressure on them to work additional hours which might interfere with their other obligations.

- What is most important to you, professionally? *(Examples might include having the chance to contribute to something important, to grow in professional confidence, to build a good reputation at work)*

- What is most important to you, personally? *(Examples might include a young family, being able to get home on time, caring for a sick relative, church group or charity work)*

ASPIRATIONS:

Aspirations are very personal and an important source of motivation. If you know what an employee wants for the future, you can help them to work towards it.

 What are your aspirations...

- Professionally? *(Examples might include getting promoted, achieving professional qualifications, high profile projects, working with experts, being mentored by someone senior)*

- Personally? *(Examples might include success in a chosen sporting league, to start a charitable foundation or raise funds for a charity, to get published or develop a singing career)*

- Where do you see yourself in five years' time? *(examples might include a senior role, going self employed, winning an industry award for contribution, or pursuing further academic study)*

COMPETENCES:

Competences may be a source of capability for you to tap into, but don't overload someone with these tasks, especially if they don't enjoy them very much.

Even if you don't particularly enjoy doing it, in which areas or tasks have you learned to become really competent?

- Professionally? *(Examples might include project planning, understanding a piece of legislation, or speaking at an industry event)*

- Personally? (*Examples might include resolving conflict at work, mediation skills, becoming a mental health first aider*)

- What have you learned to be good at, but actually don't enjoy at all? *(Examples might include copy checking, creating a knowledge database, resolving difficult customer complaints)*

EXPERIENCE

If you didn't interview this employee, you may not be aware of previous experience they have which could be really relevant to an upcoming project.

- Outline your main professional background and experience

- Which work experiences and challenges have given you the greatest satisfaction?

- Which non-work experiences have you enjoyed most?

- What do you like doing in your spare time?

- Which community activities do you support (if any)?

High Employee Engagement Leads to High Performance

Completing the SPACE analysis with each person in your team enables you to get to know them a bit better. Working with them to design the role and the workload in a way which best fits their preferences means you are likely to get higher levels of performance and engagement from them, which will lead to a more positive work environment for the team, and less time spent on Crucible Conversations for you.

Now that you have understood them as individuals, let's look at the things you could be doing to create an environment at work which is conducive to high performance.

Global research company, Gallup, specialise in measuring employee engagement at work. They have identified 12 questions – usually included as part of an employee satisfaction survey – as the key drivers of employee engagement. In other words, if an employee scores highly on each of these 12 questions, they are more likely to stay and work hard for their employer.

According to the Gallup research, up to a third of employees report feeling actively disengaged at work. A further third report feeling neither engaged nor disengaged; in other words, sometimes they feel engaged, sometimes they don't. This means that only a third (at best) report feeling actively engaged at work. These people are the only ones really working at their best, and helping an organisation to succeed.

If you are looking at your to-do list and worrying that you don't have enough people in your team to get the job done properly, the reality is possibly that you don't have sufficiently engaged people in your team, or if you do, that they are not prioritising effectively, or that issues of poor performance are going unchallenged because you are too busy to do anything about it. The higher the levels of engagement, the better the performance, and the more manageable the workload.

The good news is that you can do something about all of that!

It should be easy, but managers don't always make time for the most important elements, such as providing recognition for good performance, encouraging individual development, or explaining the significance of the work they do.

Have a look at the 12 statements on the next page, and give yourself a score out of 10 to reflect your own recent experience at work.

Activity 1.4: How Engaged are YOU?

How would you score yourself (out of a maximum of 10) against each of the Gallup 12 drivers of employee engagement?

Nr	Element	Your score / 10
1	I know what is expected of me at work	
2	I have the equipment I need to do my job	
3	I have the opportunity to do what I do best, every day at work	
4	In the last week, I have received recognition for working well	
5	Someone at work seems to care about me as a person	
6	Someone at work encourages my development	
7	At work, I feel that my opinions count	
8	The mission of my organisation makes me feel that my work is important	
9	My colleagues are committed to doing quality work	
10	I have a close friend at work	
11	In the last 6 months, someone has discussed my progress with me	
12	This last year, I have had opportunities at work to learn and grow	

There is a lot more information on the Gallup website (www.gallup.com), and their various publications explain in much more detail how you can use their research to create a high-performance organisation.

Activity 1.5: Employee Engagement Action Plan

Once you have assessed your own levels of engagement at work, ask the members of your team to do the same. It's best to ask them to do it anonymously, so that they don't feel under pressure to tell you what they think you want to hear.

Then, take a few moments to complete the personal action plan, reflecting on the 12 elements of employee engagement to ensure that you are leading by example, role modelling what excellent performance looks like at work.

What are your team's highest scoring areas?

*   _____

*   _____

How could you improve further in these areas to boost team engagement levels?

*   _____

*   _____

Which were your team's lowest scoring areas:

*   _____

*   _____

What action will you take to resolve this?

*   _____

*   _____

Don't wait for HR to take action to improve employee engagement at work. There is a lot you can be doing to make a difference, right now.

Chapter 1 personal reflections and insights

Take a moment now to reflect on what you have read in this chapter, and the exercises and activities you have completed. Be sure to extract the wisdom from your own insights, and apply it to improve your daily management practice.

- My main reasons for wanting to be a leader, are:

- As a result of reading this chapter, I now understand my obligations as a line manager, and these include:

- It is <u>not</u> HR's job to:

- I will take the following steps to understand the motivations of each person in my team:

- In terms of improving overall team engagement levels, I plan to:

Chapter Two: Setting Goals

Why Set Goals?

Research has shown that people respond well when they have clearly articulated goals. It gives us something to focus on and work towards, and there is profound satisfaction to be achieved from reaching our target. Without goals, we risk sleep-walking through life, or settling into a comfortable but boring routine where every day and every year feels the same. This is why companies set goals for business success, and teams have goals to promote team success and individual success, too.

What have been some of the most satisfying goals you have ever achieved (personally or professionally)?

-
-
-

And how did you feel when you achieved them?

- I felt...

How do you respond to identifying goals for your work, now?

- I respond by...

How does it feel when you achieve them?

- I feel...

How do the people in your team respond when you set them goals?

- They seem to feel...

Did you know... according to research published in Harvard Business Review, people who set themselves goals for their free time (see friends, sort out the garden, decorate the spare room) feel more fulfilled and report greater satisfaction and recuperation than those who just sat in front of the TV.

Aligning Individual and Organisational Goals

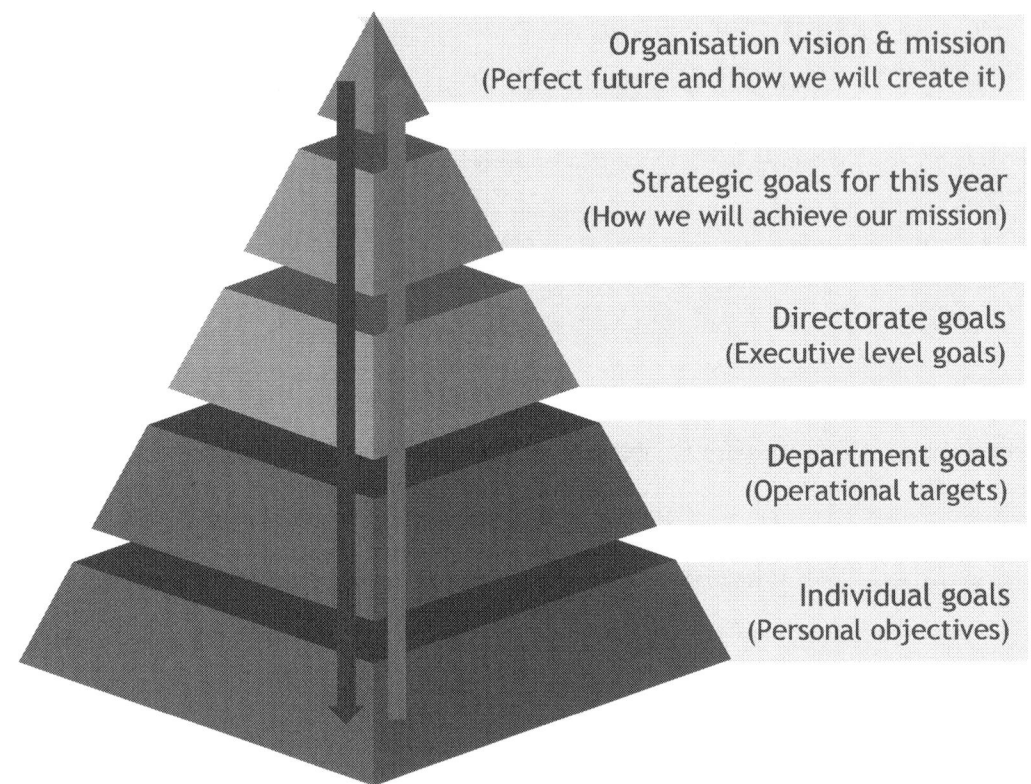

Organisation vision & mission
(Perfect future and how we will create it)

Strategic goals for this year
(How we will achieve our mission)

Directorate goals
(Executive level goals)

Department goals
(Operational targets)

Individual goals
(Personal objectives)

Employees need to feel that their goals are meaningful. Being able to link individual goals back up to department goals, and department goals up to the goals for your directorate, and the strategic goals for this year, and then ultimately to the mission of the organisation... can play a powerful role in helping people to see why their work matters, and understand where they fit into the overall success of the organisation.

Each person in your team should be able to see exactly how their work contributes to higher level business goals, and from an executive perspective, a leader wants to see those strategic goals broken down into individual tasks.

Your job as a line manager is to help your people feel valued as employees, and spelling it out to them in this way will make it easier for them to see the connection. If the team works well together already, you could ask them to work together as a team to identify and choose goals for themselves, linked to their SPACE analysis. That would be a powerful way to drive individual goal ownership and strong team cohesion. Setting positive long-term goals can really help a team to bond together.

FAQ: How many goals should I set?

Three to five business goals and at least one professional development goal is a good number to focus performance. If you try to set too many, your employee may struggle to know which to prioritise.

Sharing team goals with the team

It can be helpful to build understanding on how the workload is divided and aligned by creating a document detailing everyone's headline goals, and making it available for everyone to see. Don't include personal development or improvement goals here; that is private and confidential. When team members are aware of each other's goals, they will be more likely to share relevant information and collaborate on information gathering and reporting. Progress against these goals may be a useful conversation point at team meetings as well.

Name	Goal 1: increase customer satisfaction	Goal 2: reduce process waste	Goal 3: grow market share by 5%
Abdul	Complete annual customer satisfaction assessment for all key accounts	Plan and facilitate discussions with all business partners regarding process improvement suggestions	Research intel on emerging customer needs
Benoit	Carry out 1:1 qualitative interviews with all key client stakeholders	Run activity-based costing training sessions with all change champions	Work with strategy team to identify 'Blue Ocean' opportunities
Carl	Ensure customer delight plan is integrated with overall business improvement plan	Set special interest group on process improvement within our networking breakfast sessions	Work with legal team to develop framework agreements to secure forward business
Davide	Set up customer satisfaction action groups to drive through	Explore possibility of implementing a six sigma approach	Carry out gap analysis to identify opportunities for new business
Elena	Make tactical and strategic recommendations on how to improve customer satisfaction	Look at end-to-end customer experience data to identify non value-add activity	Research current financial viability of key competitors and report on weaknesses

FAQ: But what if the goalposts change?

As business priorities change, our competitors change, our customers change their minds, and team members come and go, some of the goals we set may become more relevant, or less so. Regular review and updating of goals will help to ensure that an employee is focusing on the most relevant tasks throughout the performance cycle.

FAQ: But I haven't received my goals from MY line manager, yet.

For all employee goals and objectives to be truly aligned in a way that will deliver the strategic aims of your business, goals should cascade from the very highest level. If you haven't received your goals yet from your line manager, ask them when you can expect them. And if they haven't received their goals yet from their line manager, raise it with their line manager. Don't worry about being a nuisance... you are trying to do your best to create high performance in your part of the organisation.

If you keep asking, but never get any answers, you can still make a decision on which goals would seem to make sense, given the strategy of your organisation. A good place to start is looking at the goals you set last year, and raising the bar a little. So, if your quality goal last year was for no more that 8% quality faults, you could aim for 5% this year.

FAQ: But nobody seems to know what our strategy is!

If you understand the nature of the business you are in, you could try developing a business strategy with your line manager, explaining that you need to be able to align team goals with business strategy.

If that doesn't work, maybe the business lacks a strategic focus. Give us a call – we can help you with that.

Activity 2.1: Linking the Goals with the SPACE analysis

If you can link the personal performance goals to the strengths, priorities, aspirations, competences and experience of each member of your team, they are much more likely to invest effort and energy to achieve them. Remember, when people get to do what they do best at work, they will perform better and enjoy their work much more.

Now, write a business-related work goal for yourself, linked to your own SPACE analysis from activity 1.3.

How can you use this process to link the SPACE analysis with performance goals for each person in your team?

Setting SMART Goals... together

Goals create a roadmap to success by helping you to define where you want to go, plan the best route, check to see how close you are to your final destination and confirm when you have arrived. Without goals, you risk doing the wrong things, focus on irrelevant tasks, and drift through life. That's not how businesses succeed, and neither will your employees succeed if they don't have goals of their own.

The best goals are **SMART** goals!

Specific: Be precise when describing what you want the employee to work on. What does success look like? How will they know when they have achieved it?
Rewrite this non-specific goal so that everyone understands what is expected:

"Improve product quality"

* _____

Measurable: What level of performance are you looking for? By making it measurable, both parties will know when it has been achieved. Rewrite this non-measurable goal so that everyone understands what is expected and how well it needs to be done:

"Reduce customer complaints"

* _____

Agreed: the employee will not own the goal until they have agreed them. How will you ensure that they agree to the goals you are setting them?

* _____

Relevant: It is not enough for the goal to be agreed; it also has to be relevant to the success of the business. How can you ensure that the employee understands the relevance of the goal you are setting them?

* _____

Time-bound: Open-ended goals are rarely achieved. Be clear about the deadline for completion of the goal. Rewrite this non-time bound goal:

"Complete the project delivery."

* _____

Activity 2.2: Writing SMART goals

Now, go back to the goal you have written for yourself in activity 2.1, and *rewrite it*, this time ensuring it is *SMART*.

Measuring Goal Achievement

You can measure the completion of a goal in different ways. Sometimes it will be obvious, and you can measure it quantitatively (i.e., in terms of absolute numbers). Other goals will be more qualitative, in other words, it may be about *how* something was achieved rather than just what. Even with goals which are harder to measure quantitatively, you should be clear with your employees exactly what 'excellent' looks like, otherwise it will just be their opinion versus yours at the end of the year review.

Activity 2.3 Quantitative Measure

Ensure that your goal has a quantitative measure of success by putting a number with it. That can be a percentage of improvement, a unit number target, or a reduction rate.

Activity 2.4 Qualitative Measure

Now, articulate a qualitative measure by saying how the goal needs to be achieved by considering measures of success such as customer satisfaction, employee engagement etc.

Chapter 2 personal reflections and insights

Take a moment now to reflect on what you have read in this chapter, and the exercises and activities you have completed. Be sure to extract the wisdom from your own insights, and apply it to improve your daily management practice.

- As a result of reading this chapter, I now understand that as a line manager, I need to ensure that:

- It is important to align individual goals with business goals because:

- The optimal number of goals I should set for each person in my team, is:

- Linking individual goals to the SPACE analysis will help me to:

- Setting SMART goals will help during performance reviews, because:

Chapter Three: Reviewing Progress

Setting goals is only the first step. Once you have agreed the goals with members of your team, you will need to schedule in some regular review time to ensure that everything is on track.

FAQ: How often should I discuss and review progress?

Most high-performance organisations have formalised their approach to goal-setting and performance management. Even if you don't have a formal process in your organisation, it will help you, your team, the organisation and your own career to create a culture of encouraging others for high performance.

Setting clear expectations for high performance should be a part of your normal day-to-day discussions with your people anyway, but industry best practice suggests that in order to help to keep goals in the forefront of their minds, having monthly one-to-one meetings is the best way to help your people stay focused. When managing high performance, you will need to check in regularly with each person to ensure that they are still focused on the right things. If you can't find the time to do this on a monthly basis, at least try to do it every six weeks.

Schedule time regularly with each person in your team; it not only enables you to focus together on progress towards goals, but also provides an important opportunity to check in with each member of the team to find out how they are.

How would a regular one-to-one with each member of your team help to sustain high performance?

-
-
-
-
-

One-to-One Meetings with Your Team

Research shows that the channel of communication which employees trust most is their line manager. They like to hear company messages explained, put into context, and made relevant to them so that they can build a clearer understanding of what they need to do to help the company to succeed.

FAQ: But I'm too busy to do that *every* month!

Many managers take the view that one-to-one meetings with each member of their team is time-consuming and unnecessary, believing that if their staff want to talk to them about something, they would do it as part of the normal course of events. This is a mistaken belief! Sometimes people feel on show if they ask for a quiet word with the boss, or see a one-to-one meeting as the place where they receive criticism. Maybe they wouldn't feel comfortable talking to you 'in passing', and would prefer some one-to-one time to discuss issues with you privately.

Clear and honest communication is a key factor in building trust and leading a high-performance team, and should be a priority for everyone with line management responsibility. What should you talk about? Here is a suggested agenda for your one-to-one meeting, so you don't have to think about what to say. You can circulate it to your team so that they know what to expect, and it gives you a logical structure to follow, so you're never stuck for things to talk about. You can take notes, or just listen. You can also schedule these meetings in advance, so everyone is clear that there are no hidden agendas.

Agenda for Monthly One-to-One Meeting

1. How's it going? – a general catch-up on current workload and responsibilities.

2. Current priorities? – make sure your people are prioritising things which are critical to the business.

3. Any issues you're currently facing? – tells you of any problems (real or anticipated) that might affect their performance, so that together, you can formulate a plan.

4. Progress with goals – this ensures that your team is focusing their efforts in the right direction, and gives you the opportunity to refocus your employee, as well as being aware of their progress and giving them ongoing feedback. It also makes the annual appraisal easier for both of you.

5. Recent messages – manager adds some context to company messages to ensure that they have been clearly understood, and that the employee knows what is expected of them.

6. Any feedback about my management style, or anything you need from me? This helps you to tackle any interpersonal issues proactively, rather than leaving it until there is a problem.

7. Anything else you want to tell me? A final catch-all to give the employee the chance to raise personal or interpersonal issues not previously mentioned.

8. Thanks! Your opportunity to give your employee some positive feedback to help them feel valued and respected.

Any other questions you would add to make this a positive and supportive conversation?

- _____
- _____
- _____

Conducting a Formal Review Meeting in the Right Frame of Mind

Look to the formal review meeting as an opportunity to refocus or redirect your employee, and give them the chance to develop and grow. This will make the meeting much more constructive than if you see it as an opportunity to download a heap of criticism.

Formal review of progress usually happens at mid-year review, and end-of-year appraisal. Sometimes, it needs to happen at a different time, for example in the case of consistent poor performance which may lead to disciplinary action or termination of employment. There are many reasons that people may struggle to achieve business objectives and goals, some of which you will know about, and others maybe you won't. Start your meeting from a place of mutual respect and aim to try to identify together any issues which may be blocking the performance of an individual.

Earlier, we looked at the SPACE analysis. You may find it useful to revisit it ahead of the meeting in order to remind yourself of the employee's strengths, priorities, aspirations, competences and experience. They will have joined your organisation hoping to do a good job and maybe to progress their career, so they won't want to fail, and will appreciate your support.

List below some operational or personal issues which may be getting in the way, and consider how you would respond to each of these if they are raised during the discussion.

Operational issues: Response:

Personal issues: Response:

Checking in on your own Unconscious Bias

We all make snap judgements about people, and form opinions through our own filters on the world. It's hard (but not impossible) to update those filters, and judge others as kindly as we hope they will judge us. But we must be aware of unconscious bias when measuring and managing the performance of our people.

Have you ever met someone for the first time, and immediately liked them? This is called the 'affinity bias', and is usually because they remind you of someone else you know and like. It will influence your feelings and opinions of them every time you meet them or work with them. Have you ever met someone for the first time, and taken an instant dislike to them? It's called the 'horn effect' and may be because subconsciously they remind you of someone else you didn't like. But you then treat them as someone you don't like, and it affects every single interaction with them. Worse still, if we have made a snap judgement about someone (and we *all* do it!), they will have to work hard to change that judgement, because we tend only to notice information that confirms the judgement we have already made. That is 'confirmation bias'.

If you like or dislike someone, it will be subtly communicated in every interaction – the warmth of your smile, the attention you pay, your body language, the words you use, what you say about them to others, and the feedback you give. When you know someone doesn't like you (no matter how well they try to hide it), you will sense it, and will be less willing to help, less forgiving of their mistakes, less complimentary when talking about them, and generally be less cooperative when working with them.

As managers, you will undoubtedly have opinions about each person in your team. It's called 'observer bias'. But are those opinions fair, or are you making judgements through the filter of your own biases? Be honest with yourself: is this person really under-performing, or is it that *you* just don't like them?

For example, is this employee's attention to detail *really* disastrous, or is it just that they made a mistake recently, and it has affected your judgement of them. Beware of 'recency bias', where you recall only a recent example or incident, and make that the whole story about someone's capability.

Is their attention to detail *really* poor, or is it just that YOU are excellent at the detail, whereas the other person is more of a strategic thinker? Be aware of 'in-group bias', where you tend to treat people more favourably when they are the same as you.

Preparing for a Formal Review

The formal review process will be a structured conversation around how an employee has performed against the goals set at the start of the year. This meeting is usually part of the annual performance cycle – maybe a midyear review, or the end of year appraisal. Check with HR that you are following the company procedure correctly.

A formal review will usually look at attitude and behaviour (the 'how') as well as achievement of goals (the 'what'). The first element can be harder to prove than the second, so make sure you have done sufficient preparation.

Possible evidence of attitude and behaviour

- Time keeping
- Completion of specific requests
- Willingness to go the extra mile
- Use of own initiative
- Reputation with other managers or leadership team
- Response to pressure, or behaviour when stressed
- Courtesy and willingness to help others
- Dealing with conflict with a colleague
- Response to feedback
- *Others?*
-

Possible evidence of performance

- Completion of goals
- Achievement of additional tasks and activities
- Milestones met
- Quality standards achieved and maintained
- Customer feedback received (include internal and external customers)
- Attitude and performance as a team player
- *Others?*
-

When under-performance is an ongoing problem with a specific employee, you will need to articulate a clear performance improvement plan (sometimes referred to as a 'PIP') to help them to reach the required level of performance, spelling out exactly what changes are required, and the consequences of failing to improve. This is your job, as a line manager, and they should be expecting it. If it helps, you can refer them to the appropriate HR procedure, drawing their attention to any element which indicates your role – and theirs – in the performance management process.

If you have discussed performance and progress at regular informal check-ins, there should be no nasty surprises for either of you.

Tip: Have your evidence to hand for when the review begins, so that you can back up your comments and observations appropriately.

Logistics: Right Place, Right Time

Always make sure that a progress review meeting is carried out in private. Book a meeting room or find a quiet office and schedule the time in your – and their – calendar. It will help to book the meeting for longer than you actually need, just in case the conversation gets complicated, or the other person needs time to deal with some difficult emotions. You can start with an hour, but if you anticipate it might take longer, then book the meeting room for two hours instead. That should give you plenty of time.

It can be tempting to delay the review meeting until after the weekend / Christmas, or after their / your holiday, but the longer you put it off, the more it will prey on your mind. Schedule the review for as soon as possible, and leave it for the employee to reflect upon the conversation upon over the break, and to decide how to respond.

Keep a Record of the Conversation

During a formal review, you will need to record careful notes of the conversation for your file. You may need to refer to them at a later stage, particularly if you end up having to terminate someone's employment because of persistent poor performance.

It will help to note the date and time of the review meeting, the issues raised, any supporting evidence you gathered, how the employee responded to feedback, any concerns raised or mitigating circumstances declared, and the agreed action plan.

It will really help you and your direct report to frame your discussions as an invitation to grow and develop, rather than seeing it as a way to deliver criticism. Using language like "Good... even better if..." will get you off to the right start, and will reduce the likelihood of the other person becoming defensive. There's more on finding exactly the right words to say in chapter 4.

In summary, prepare carefully for a formal review; gather your evidence, book a meeting room, give the other person plenty of time to prepare, practise the words you want to say, work to achieve your desired outcome, and follow up after the meeting.

40% preparation
+
20% meeting
+
40% follow-up action
=
100% successful review meeting

Define your desired outcomes from the meeting: Think, Feel, Do

When preparing for an informal or formal review, it will really help you to plan ahead to get a good outcome from your conversation.

Take a moment to consider an answer to these three questions when you are preparing for a conversation with a team member.

THINK: what do you want the other person to think as a result of this conversation?
- That you like them
- That you respect them
- That you value their opinion
-
-

FEEL: How do you want them to feel as a result of this conversation?

- Supported?
- Recognised?
- Trusted?
-
-

DO: What do you want them to do differently as a result of the conversation?

- Prioritise more effectively
- Work harder / smarter
- Use more professional language when talking to colleagues
-
-

When you start the conversation with a clear outcome in mind, it will be much easier to determine if the message landed as intended.

How to Rate Performance

If your organisation uses a formal process and template for managing performance, it is likely that they will offer specific guidance on how to rate individual performance.

Some organisations use a 1 – 5 rating scale (where 5 is very high, and 1 is very low).

Others use worded scales, such as:

- Regularly exceeds expectations
- Fully meets expectations
- Partially meets expectations
- Fails to meet some expectations
- Fails to meet all expectations

It may be tempting to give each person in the team a high score because you want to remain on good terms with everyone. The problem here is that it might appear that you are unable to differentiate between excellent performance and ordinary or even poor performance. Likewise, it would be difficult to justify giving high scores to each individual if you are missing your team targets overall.

It is better to be honest with yourself and with your team members. For clarity, it can help you to reflect honestly on their performance by sorting them into a list of highest performer to lowest performer. Then, be sure to differentiate clearly when rating them.

When it comes to giving the feedback, however, treat each person as an individual, and don't verbally compare the performance of one person with that of their colleagues. It can breed resentment and accusations of favouritism.

Forced Distribution

Some organisations will opt for forced distribution when rating staff performance. This means that you are forced to distribute a balance of highest and lowest grades throughout the team. This tends to happen when managers are too soft on scoring performance, so be honest and set clear expectations as soon as you can. The example below shows how a manager might apply forced distribution to individual performance appraisals in a team of 10 people, and the course of action they might select as a consequence.

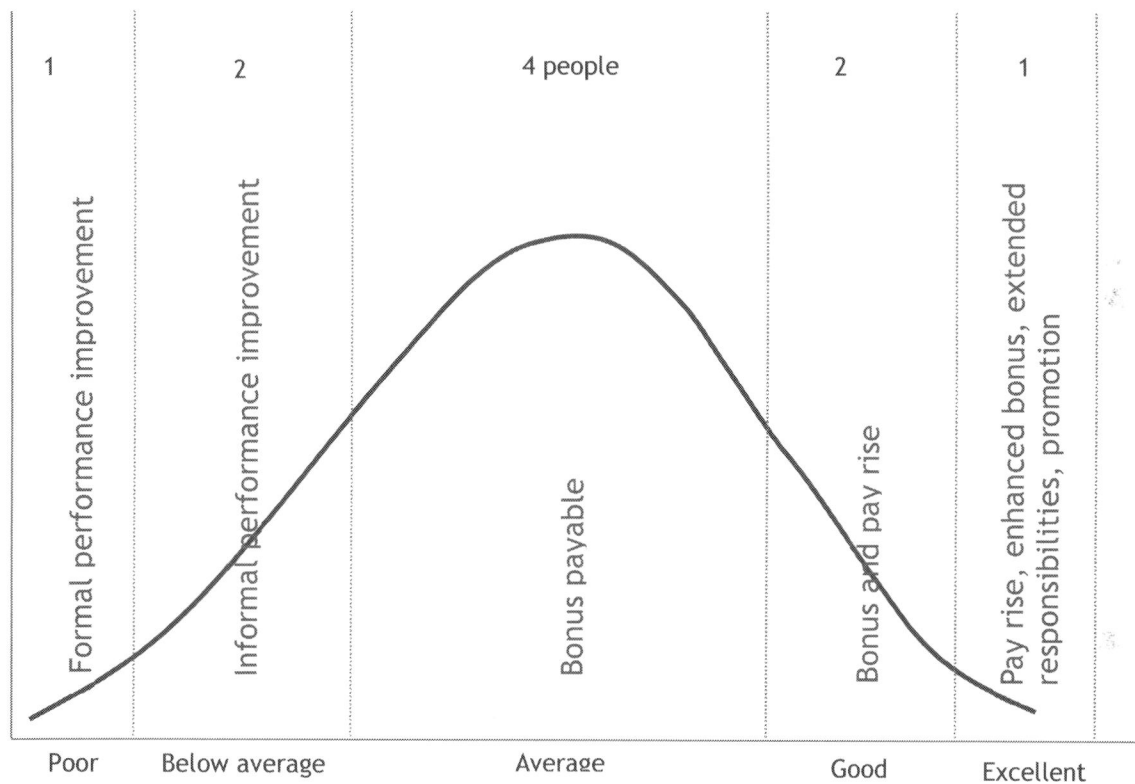

Step Reviews

Also known as grandparent reviews, some organisations will require you to get your team scores double-checked by another manager. This is designed to reduce any possible bias, and is good practice for ensuring a fair review process, but it is quite time-consuming. However, two heads are better than one, so embrace any opportunity to hear another perspective. Even if it isn't a formal part of the performance management process, it can be useful to ask your line manager if they want to add anything.

FAQ: What if an employee disagrees with the rating?

Some employees may have a different perception of their capability, and you may find yourself having to justify the ratings you have allocated. The evidence you collected ahead of the performance review will help you to back up your position. HR may be able to provide further guidance on this, according to your company policy. You should make a note on file that the employee disagreed with your rating, as it could be helpful in the event of a grievance.

Managing and Motivating for High Performance: Willing & Able

Sometimes, despite all the support you give them, your employees just don't perform as well as you had hoped. There is a number of possible reasons for that:

- They don't like the work
- They cannot do the work
- They are overloaded with work, and feel that they can't cope
- They have problems outside of work which affect their concentration
- They don't have a good relationship with their co-workers
- They don't have a good relationship with their line manager
- They don't understand the significance / relevance of the work
- The work doesn't play to their strengths
- They are disengaged, bored, or looking for another job
- They disagree with how the work has been allocated

The matrix below acknowledges the different attitudes that you might observe from people in your team. Knowing where they are on this grid can give you a really helpful steer on how to manage them in a way that best suits their development needs and encourages them to do their very best.

Willing but Unable | Willing & Able

Unwilling & Unable | Unwilling, but Able

Willing & Able:

These are usually among your best performers. They know what is expected of them and will get on with doing the job to the standard you require. Even though they're already doing a great job, everyone needs a bit of recognition and encouragement to help keep them motivated, so don't ignore these people.

Willing but Unable:

These people may be new to the team or the business, and are slowly picking up speed and making good progress, but they're not quite there yet. They will probably need a bit more of your time and support, although they are willing and eager to learn. Try some training or buddying – especially from someone else in the team who is already good at the same task. And give them plenty of encouragement so that they don't feel defeated if they make a mistake.

Unwilling, but Able:

These people may have been in the company for a long time, and might have become bored or frustrated. They have lots of knowledge and experience, but have lost the enthusiasm. Interestingly, people in this quadrant will often be able to offer support and guidance to people who are Willing-but-Unable, thereby reigniting their own interest.

Unwilling & Unable:

It's very easy to give up on these people, especially if you've spent a lot of time trying to support them, but nothing really seems to work. But they were good once, otherwise they wouldn't have got the job. Find out what these people are really good at and interested in (see the SPACE analysis to find out what's important to them). These people can often be moved to the Willing & Able quadrant with a change in role or responsibilities. Don't ignore them, otherwise their colleagues will think that there are no consequences for poor performance!

One more thing:

The Willing & Able matrix is a great way to understand what is going on for each member of your team. Take a moment to reflect on how your attitude towards your people may be affecting their performance, too. If you think that someone in your team is not competent, then even without realising it, you will be communicating that message to them, and that in itself will impact on their motivation. It can become a vicious circle.

Ask yourself instead about their strengths and experiences, and how you could focus on those as a springboard to improving performance.

Strategies for Managing the People in Your Team

Below, you will see some proven strategies for managing each person in your team, whatever their current levels of willingness and ability.

Willing but Unable? Develop!	Willing & Able? Delegate!
✓ Train/coach/mentor ✓ Buddy with another team member ✓ Communicate your trust ✓ Provide regular encouragement ✓ Celebrate progress ✗ Don't ignore them ✗ Don't overstretch them ✗ Don't criticise or compare them to others in the team	✓ Provide greater autonomy ✓ Give recognition & encouragement ✓ Provide stretch goals and maybe some people management experience ✗ Don't ignore them ✗ Don't overload them ✗ Do NOT take them for granted
Unwilling & Unable? Redirect!	Unwilling, but Able? Engage!
✓ Find out why they are unwilling ✓ Do strengths / personality testing: are they in the right job? ✓ Help them understand consequences ✗ Don't ignore or tolerate ✗ Don't just fire them (even if it's tempting!) ✗ Don't let them infect other team members	✓ Do SPACE analysis to understand what's important to them ✓ Give recognition and encouragement ✓ Coach them ✓ Maybe ask them to mentor someone ✗ Don't ignore or side line them ✗ Don't rely on financial incentives (improvement will be temporary)

Activity 3.1: Managing My Team

Thinking back to your team, now, which position best describes their current will and ability?

Transfer the names of the people in your team onto the grid below so that you have a clear perspective on the nature of your performance management challenge.

Once you've added the names, identify some specific strategies and tactics to help move them up into the 'willing and able' category.

Willing, but Unable? Develop!	Willing & Able? Delegate!
Unwilling, Unable? Redirect!	**Unwilling, but Able? Engage!**

Honesty and Respect: delivering feedback with professionalism

Any feedback you provide must be constructive, and delivered with an appropriate level of respect and honesty to ensure that the message is understood. In an ideal world, all feedback would be delivered with high respect and high honesty, but sometimes we get it wrong. We can all think of examples of bad feedback!

HIGH	**High respect/ low honesty** Manager gives feedback but dodges the real issue	**High respect/ high honesty** Manager gives honest feedback in a respectful, constructive way.
RESPECT	**Low respect/ low honesty** Manager is avoidant and blunt when pressed	**Low respect/ high honesty** Manager gives honest feedback but in a critical way.
LOW		
	LOW **HONESTY** HIGH	

What are the consequences of feedback delivered with...?

HIGH respect, but LOW honesty:

- _____

LOW respect, but HIGH honesty:

- _____

LOW honesty and LOW respect:

- _____

How will you prepare to give your feedback with HIGH RESPECT and HIGH HONESTY?

- _____

Low respect, low honesty

Here, the manager does not give honest feedback, and is not respectful. They throw out unsubstantiated criticism, creating anger, resentment and disengagement. The result is that they develop a reputation as a bully, insensitive, and with low emotional intelligence. That can really limit your career!

Low respect, high honesty

The manager gives blunt feedback to the employee. It may be honest feedback but it is not delivered in a respectful way. This too can create resentment, anger and frustration, and is likely to result in some verbal retaliation, or a heated argument.

High respect, low honesty

The manager gives feedback, but it is not fully honest. Instead, they tiptoe around the subject and avoid being specific in order to reduce the risk of conflict or discomfort. The result is that the employee thinks they are performing better than they are, and will start to expect a pay rise, bonuses and a promotion. They will be confused when that doesn't happen.

High respect, high honesty

In the best case, the manager will provide honest feedback in a respectful, constructive way. The employee will understand clearly what is expected of them, and even if some of the feedback is hard to hear, they will likely be more open to discussing a route to improvement.

Tip: what you don't challenge, you condone! If you start to see problems of attitude, behaviour and performance among members of your team, you will need to address it quickly. It is your job, and they are expecting you to do it.

FAQ: But what if I actually just need to fire them?

There will be occasions in your line management career where terminating someone's contract of employment is the best thing for everyone concerned. However, it can also be one of the most traumatic things that ever happens to that person, especially if they are supporting a family which will suffer real hardship as a result of losing an income.

Perhaps you have experienced being fired at some point early on in your career. If you have, you will understand the importance of a manager getting straight to the point and saying what they mean. An employee may be in shock when they first hear the bad news, and might have struggled to take in the finer details of the situation. At times like this, having a written confirmation of the decision taken by the company and the reasons will be really helpful, especially if it includes things such as any pay in lieu of notice, or unused holiday, and any financial settlement such as a redundancy payment or compromise agreement. Written confirmation will also outline the notice period they will be required to work, or if they are to be put on 'gardening leave', which usually means that although their employment is terminated with immediate effect, they are contractually bound not to work for a competitor within a certain period of time after leaving. This will have been outlined in their initial contract of employment, and shouldn't come as a surprise. The letter would also usually cover things like returning company property, such as computer, phone, car, keys.

If their work is commercially sensitive, you can ask security staff to supervise them clearing their desk and then escort them off the premises immediately. This is usually done to prevent access to commercially sensitive information, or damage to company property. It is an extremely humiliating experience, however, and it may be best while this is happening, to invite their colleagues into another meeting room where you will brief them on what has happened. This makes things less embarrassing for everyone.

Once the person has left the premises, you will want to notify the rest of the organisation. It would be wholly inappropriate to detail any of the reasons for their departure, and most make a generic statement along the lines of "With immediate effect, this person has now left the organisation to pursue a career elsewhere. We wish them luck in their future endeavours." HR can advise you on what to say.

You do need to make some sort of announcement, however. If people just 'disappear', it can be extremely unsettling to everyone who remains, and the rumour mill will likely be working overtime, speculating on what happened, and worrying about who is next.

HR will advise you on all of these areas, and it is <u>imperative</u> that you follow their guidance exactly to reduce the likelihood of legal action against the organisation.

Chapter 3 personal reflections and insights

Take a moment now to reflect on what you have read in this chapter, and the exercises and activities you have completed. Be sure to extract the wisdom from your own insights, and apply it to improve your daily management practice.

- There are many benefits to scheduling a regular informal review with each person in my team, such as:

- Giving inflated feedback to people in my team will cause problems by:

- Hitting the right balance of honesty and respect during formal reviews will help to:

- Preparation before and follow-up after a performance review can add up to 80% of the successful outcome, because:

- Firing team members who are both unable and unwilling to improve their performance and attitude should be a last resort, because:

Chapter Four: Navigating a Crucible Conversation™

A Crucible Conversation is a discussion with another individual where they – and possibly you – need to face up to some difficult truths. In metalworking terms, a crucible is a container in which metals are heated to a very high temperature, changing the structure of the contents so that it can be reformed and reshaped into something new. A Crucible Conversation then, is a challenging conversation where each party has the choice to stick rigidly to their perspective and choices, or to heed the feedback, and make different decisions which may change their entire life outcomes. Crucible Conversations always bring an invitation to change, and to refine and refocus our efforts. Even though many people dread such testing situations, they can be the making of an individual, and they may one day look back to the moment of a particularly challenging Crucible Conversation, and be grateful that it happened.

Managers may avoid having Crucible Conversations at work for a number of reasons. Often, they are not sure of their facts, and are afraid to make unfounded accusations. If this applies to you, the simple answer is to do your homework in advance of a conversation, and have your evidence to hand.

Some managers doubt the legitimacy of the Crucible Conversation, or their right to deliver a difficult message. Others suspect that they should have already fixed the problem themselves. But as a manager, you will not have time to do all the work yourself; you will need to rely on the people in your team, and not only is it your right to challenge your staff, they will also be expecting it of you, because you are the manager, and they will lose respect for you if you don't.

The main reason that managers avoid having Crucible Conversations about performance at work is that they are afraid the other person will take the criticism badly, and the situation will quickly escalate, resulting in an argument or accusations of bullying and harassment.

No matter how difficult the topic, knowing the right words to say will help you to navigate such a conversation with professionalism and poise, and is less likely to end up in a heated argument involving HR.

Take a moment to think back to your own career. Can you recall a Crucible Conversation which made you see the world differently, and as a result, made different choices?

A Crucible Conversation can be a very helpful intervention!

Levels of Crucible Conversation™

- ## Level 1 (Low conflict) A friendly, informal conversation

As a simple rule of thumb, following the 'good... even better if' structure helps to keep the conversation on a positive level, and is less likely to result in defensiveness.

- ## Level 2 (Potential conflict) A more challenging conversation

When faced with the evidence of poor performance, undesirable attitudes or inconsistent attendance, some people will quickly become angry or tearful. It's a defence mechanism, designed to make the problem go away, and incredibly, will probably stem from some early childhood emotional conditioning. (The point at which a parent gives into their child's demands is the point at which the child learns how to get their own way; if crying makes the parent give in to the request for sweets, then the child learns to cry to get what they want. If having a huge tantrum is what finally makes the parent relent, the child learns that tantrums are a quicker way to get their needs met. Children are not master-manipulators; they are just trying to figure out what will work for them.) Incredibly, then, those same childhood techniques which worked so well when they were young may have unwittingly become their go-to tactic for dealing with things that feel outside of their control. One thing is very likely: if the employee is shouting or crying, it will almost certainly be a mask for fear, used to distract you from their insecurities. Fear is a hugely compelling emotion, and can lead to sudden and unexpected outbursts. Whilst it may feel like an uphill struggle dealing with an employee who seems to revert to tears when the going gets tough, this section will help you to stop reinforcing that behaviour, and to make sure you stay in control of the situation. Likewise, a shouting employee can feel hugely intimidating, but it is extremely unlikely that they will resort to a physical attack because that would seal their fate and pretty much guarantee immediate termination of employment. Again, this section outlines words to use which will de-escalate a heated discussion in a way that takes the sting out of the situation without a power struggle.

1. **Deal with the emotion, first**

    When someone is shouting or crying at you, this is their raw response to their discomfort. Until you acknowledge that emotional response, you will not be able to move past it. One thing is for sure: the words 'CALM DOWN!' will never serve you, here; nobody was ever calmer as a result of being told to calm down. You can strike those words from your vocabulary – they will not help. Likewise, don't enter into an argument with the other person, because they may be much better at arguing than you, and you will lose all credibility. Your job is not to win the fight, but to reason with the other person to accept the feedback and choose to improve their performance or behaviour. An escalating argument is a sign you no longer hold the power, and that makes it much harder for you to resolve.

2. "I can see you are very angry."

Use these words when the other person is raising their voice and becoming angry. Don't say "I can see you are very upset" if they are showing anger because they are likely to correct you in the strongest words possible. Tone of voice is all important here, too. If you sound patronising or condescending, it is likely to add fuel to the flames. If your tone is dismissive or you are rolling your eyes or shaking your head, the other person will likely feel insulted, and again, the flames grow higher. Instead, maintain calm, adult-to-adult eye contact, and state clearly that you can see they are angry. A fairly deadpan delivery of the line can help. This tells them, yep, I get it; you're angry. It's usually enough to make them stop a moment, especially if this is a new tactic from you.

If the difficult conversation is one that has prompted tears from the other person, then the process is the same, except you would substitute the words "I can see you are very *upset*" and possibly use a slightly softer tone, but again, don't be patronising. If the other person thinks they have pressed your buttons and you are responding in a very soft and gentle way, backing down to de-escalate, it will reinforce the behaviour, and continue to be their go-to response when conversations become uncomfortable. Don't get drawn into their drama.

3. "Perhaps in your position, I might feel the same."

When you say this, they may hear "You're right to feel that way" ... except that that wasn't what you said. But they feel validated, and having your frustrations validated is one of the most powerful and emotionally intelligent ways to manage a situation like this. Once you have landed this line, pause a moment so that they can take stock.

4. "Help me to understand what's going on for you."

This gives the other person their chance to speak, to vent, and to list out everything that is bringing them to this emotional response. Just listen, without interrupting, and without passing judgement. This is their drama; it's not for you to decide – at this point – if their frustrations are justified.
Note, when you use the word 'why?' you are telling the other person to justify themselves. The phrase "help me to understand" is much less provocative.

5. Make a list.

   If they mention it, write it down, to show that you are listening, and also to help you work through and address each of their frustrations in turn.

6. Read it back to them.

   This demonstrates that you were listening. Once you have reached the end, ask, "Did I miss anything out?" This carries a different weight to "Is that all?" which sounds dismissive. If they mention anything else, add it in, and read the list out again.

7. "Let's see what we can do about each of these things, now."

   Once you have been through this process, it will have taken all the heat out of their anger, and will enable you both to proceed with a discussion on how to move forward. Go through each item on their list, being clear about which things you can influence, and which ones you can't. Sometimes you discover that the main reasons for the other person's frustrations lie with things entirely outside of your or their control, and sometimes those things have nothing to do with work anyway. Redirecting them to an employee assistance scheme, or gently suggesting that maybe other professional support (such as a coach, a therapist, or other advisory organisation) might be their best option, will save you from getting embroiled in their personal situation. Even though you may want to help, it will make managing their poor performance much more difficult for you if you start getting involved.

8. Agree what is in your control (as manager), and make notes on what steps you will take. You can email your commitment to the employee, so that they know exactly what to expect from you. Then do it; be true to your word.

9. Agree what action they need to take. If they haven't brought a pen and notepad, find one for them, and ask them to make some notes. If they tell you they don't need to, and that they will remember, ask them to make notes anyway. Once they have their notes, ask them to read their notes back to you so that you can be sure they have understood what they need to do. Then ask them to go back to their desk and send you an email, listing out their agreed actions. DO NOT do that part for them! Don't give them a copy of your notes, either, and don't send the email with the list of actions. Until they write them down and commit to them in writing, they won't own those actions, and can easily deny the discussion at a future date. If the email they send only lists some of the actions

discussed, ask them to write a new email to you containing the full list of actions which were agreed. You might need to remind them.

10. Thank them. When you are able to end your meeting on a positive note, shaking hands, warm smile, they feel reassured that no matter how uncomfortable the conversation has been, you have treated them fairly and with respect, and they are much more likely to engage in a positive way in future conversations.

When the other person sees that instead of backing down, you stay with the conversation until it has reached a constructive conclusion, they will stop relying on that strong emotional response to derail the process, and those conversations will become much easier in future.

• Level 3: (High conflict) The conversation is spiralling out of control

In the unlikely event that the previous words don't bring the situation back under your control, and instead, the other person raises their voice, getting more and more irate, maybe shouting, gesticulating, and threatening you, you still have options which don't result in you losing your nerve, or teeth.

"Oh, that's interesting..."

This one will likely come as a surprise, and will make them stop to hear what you are going to say next. Pause a moment to let your words sink in. Initially, they may feel justified in their outburst. Then you follow up with this:

"..why would you think it's OK to speak to me like that?"

Delivered in a cold, calm and emotionally deadpan way, the two parts of this response will usually completely disarm the most furious employee. Pause to let the words sink in.

"I am trying to help you to resolve this situation, and you appear not to want to do the same. We can do this informally, right now, or we can make it formal, and involve HR, which will go on your employee record. Tell me right now which course of action you want."

Specific Crucible Conversations™

Austrian doctor and family therapist Alfred Adler suggested that you should never chastise a child without using the opportunity to enhance their self-esteem at the same time. Some parents do this brilliantly well: "Johnny, that was a really unkind thing you did there. That's not like you! You are a kind and wonderfully thoughtful child, who is much better than that. What will you do differently next time?"

Here are some other words you might like to practise when preparing for a difficult conversation, covering a wide range of awkward topics. Let's see how using the language of positive assumptions can help to make a difficult conversation easier.

- **Body Odour**

"This is awkward, so I'm just going to get straight to the point. Your clothes don't smell very fresh. I have no doubt that you shower regularly, and that your personal hygiene is good, but I suspect that your laundry detergent isn't up to the job. Can I recommend that this weekend, you put all your work clothes through a really hot wash with a biological detergent, and send any non-machine washable items to the dry cleaners. You might even want to go into town and buy a couple of new shirts. How you smell doesn't affect your competence, but it does affect (and is affecting) how comfortable others feel working with you, and as a valued member of this team, I cannot allow that to become a problem for you."

- **Timekeeping**

"Looking at the clocking-in data, I am noticing that you have been late into work a few times recently. I know you to be a very committed and professional colleague, and that's not like you at all! Is there something we need to talk about? Let's get this sorted – I would hate for other people to draw the wrong conclusions about your timekeeping."

- **Good performance, poor attitude / behaviour**

"Let's discuss your recent performance on XYZ project. I know that this is a real area of expertise and I am delighted to have you on the team. Getting the job done well is crucial to the success of this project, and I have no concerns whatsoever about what you have achieved. But we need to discuss how you go about achieving it. I am hearing several reports about late submissions, process workarounds which breach our regulatory obligations (or health & safety rules), and abrupt and discourteous customer service. This absolutely cannot continue. People's memories are poor – they won't remember that you did a good job, they will only remember that you came across as rude or unprofessional, and that will end up hurting your career."

- ## Poor Performance

"Let's discuss this report that you have kindly pulled together. Here are the things that I really like about it; its strong points, good grammar and excellent structure. But this section looks a bit shaky, and I think we have more up to date information available for this section here.   In addition, whilst the first three parts are well written, the recommendations section – which is where you can add most value – is a bit light, and doesn't reflect your expertise. In summary, this report isn't bad, and if I had received it from anyone else in the business, I might think it was good enough. But I know you are capable of much better work than this, and I want you to take it away and rework the sections we have discussed to ensure that this is the very best example of your capability."

- ## Poor performance, poor attitude

"We need to sit down and properly evaluate some of the challenges you are facing right now. Once upon a time, you were the very best of all the candidates we interviewed, and that's why we offered you the job.   With all your years of knowledge and experience, we should be seeing much better performance from you. Help me to understand what's going on for you?"

Note: Everybody is brilliant at something, and this person might simply be in the wrong job. Take care not to be too judgemental – it may have been a management oversight to place this employee in their current role. Go back to their SPACE analysis and see how you could better redirect their efforts.

"I think it would be really useful for us to do some strengths assessments and personality profiling with you. I know you'll be brilliant at lots of things, and I am just wondering if this role isn't the best use of your talents."

- ## Broken Promises

"At our meeting on (date), you agreed to complete a series of actions designed to address the performance issues we have been discussing. Despite that reassurance from you, I am not seeing enough progress. I will fight to keep you in my team as long as I continue to believe that you are a strong and capable contributor. But you need to help me. I want you to go back to your desk right now, and send me an email listing all the actions we have agreed, and stating your commitment to complete them ahead of our next review meeting, which will be at the same time next week. I need you to understand that if you don't complete those actions, I will begin a formal performance improvement process with you, as laid out in our HR policy."

When you ask an employee to email you written confirmation of the actions they have agreed to take, you have the equivalent of a signed commitment to do the work. That way, if they still don't complete their actions, they have then broken their own promises. This is the point at which you involve someone from your Human Resources team, and begin a formal performance improvement process, or personal improvement plan (often referred to as a PIP).

Note: if you begin a formal performance improvement process (i.e., which could lead to termination of employment), you will need to take detailed and accurate notes for your records. Do it while the conversation is still fresh in your mind, in case their version of events differs wildly from yours.

Swearing

When faced with a threat, some people may resort to using more 'industrial' language as a way to vent their anger and frustration, and you need to be ready for that. No matter how tempting it may be, or how extensive your own 'industrial vocabulary', DO NOT enter into a swearing competition with another person at work. Just don't. If you swear back at them and they raise a grievance with HR about your behaviour and language, it will go on your record that you used abusive language during a review, no matter how provoked you might have felt. When they are listing out their frustrations – and you are writing them down – you can and should include specific words that they have used, to show you were listening, even if those words are not words you would use. It demonstrates that you are not intimidated by foul language, but you have noted it down for the record.

What other words and phrases have you heard that are really effective at addressing issues of performance, behaviour and attitude?

FAQ: But shouldn't these conversations be HR's job?

Go back to p9 and look again at the list of tasks which are <u>your</u> responsibility. To say this is HR's job is like saying it is the school's job to teach your children good manners. It's yours, and it goes with the territory of being a line manager.

Activity 4.1: Crucible Conversations™ with Your Team

Go back to the list of people in your team. Which conversation would help them to refocus on the right work at the right pace and at the right standard, right now?

- Person:

Crucible conversation:

- Person:

Crucible conversation:

- Person:

Crucible conversation:

- Person:

Crucible conversation:

- Person:

Crucible conversation:

- Person:

Crucible conversation:

- Person:

Crucible conversation:

Chapter 4 personal reflections and insights

Take a moment now to reflect on what you have read in this chapter, and the exercises and activities you have completed. Be sure to extract the wisdom from your own insights, and apply it to improve your daily management practice.

- As a result of reading this chapter, I now understand my obligations as a line manager include having (rather than avoiding) Crucible Conversations, which will help my team to:

- The most pressing Crucible Conversation for me right now is with _____ and is about:

- I now know that I can de-escalate a heated conversation by saying:

- Two words which I will never use again in a heated discussion, are:

Chapter Five: Coaching for Performance

Coaching as a management practice has been acknowledged by the Chartered Institute of Personnel and Development as having the potential to increase performance by as much as **80%**. As a driver of improved performance, it is being used by more and more organisations as the single most effective way to get an employee to accept and own personal goals and plans for improvement. It can be used to reinforce training and embed company messages (such as health & safety) and is at its most effective when the coach asks enough questions to help the person being coached to come up with all the answers for themselves.

The coaching process tends to follow this 6-point structure:

1. Accepting/outlining the challenge
2. Determine immediate actions that give most value
3. Agreeing actions
4. First step commitment
5. Planned activity
6. Deadline & feedback

Ask or tell?

By adopting an 'Ask' rather than 'Tell' style, a coaching manager will encourage the people in their teams to come up with their own solutions, and thereby to build confidence in their own ideas.

Which is your default style? Is it helping your team to think for themselves?

How could a coaching style of management help to improve performance in your team?

_____

_____

_____

Activity 5.1: The Spider in the Bath.

It's Sunday night – bath time! - before school in the morning, and your child comes running to find you, squealing at the top of their voice:

"There's a SPIDER in the bath!!"

How would you respond?

   a) Kill it! Job done.
   b) Just move the spider yourself – there's nothing to be afraid of
   c) Tell your child to grow up and deal with it for themselves.
   d) Show your child the 'glass-and-postcard' technique.
   e) Ask your child for their ideas on how to get rid of the spider together?

What are the possible consequences for the child for each of these options?

   a)

   b)

   c)

   d)

   e)

On reflection, what would seem to be the best option in the long term?

Activity 5.2: Don't Jump into 'Solutions' Mode!

When a manager tells an employee the solution to a problem – instead of coaching them to find their own solution - there are a number of possible consequences.

How many can you identify?

-
-
-
-
-
-
-

FAQ: But it's quicker to do it myself

Maybe, but they won't learn from that, and will begin to think that you don't trust them if you just take the task off them.

Remember: People are much more committed to their own ideas

Attitudes to Coaching

In order for coaching to be really effective, the other person needs to have the right attitude towards being coached. Take a moment to reflect on the people in your team. How would you describe their...

- **Willingness to learn?**
- **Openness to feedback?**
- **Understanding of the process?**
- **Desire to change performance or behaviour?**
- **Ability to be honest with themselves, as well as with you?**

Ready for Coaching

When the person in your team is ready, willing and interested in how coaching can help them to raise their game, they will see coaching as an opportunity to improve and exceed expectations. However, you may find on occasions that somebody is really good at seeming to agree with the need for change, but never actually gets around to implementing the actions and improvements you have discussed. They may be very good at giving excuses or saying that everything is fine now. Watch out for 'smoke screen' language / behaviour... it is often a sign of some defensiveness, a lack of clarity or fear about the outcome of the conversation.

If coaching fails to improve performance, it could be for several reasons:

- The manager fails to make enough time to coach properly
- The manager wasn't sufficiently clear about the consequences of not improving
- The goals were not clearly defined at the start
- The coach tries to solve the issue for them, leading to lack of ownership
- Milestones get missed for reasons outside of their control
- There is a lack of trust or rapport between coaching manager and employee
- There is a lack of commitment by employee
- There is a lack of honesty by employee
- *Other reasons?*
-
-

Use this as a checklist to ensure you have done everything you can before moving to a formal performance improvement discussion.

Tip: Always be clear with an employee as to why you believe coaching to be a good idea. If they trust your motives, they are more likely to engage in the process.

Coaching with the GROW model

When reviewing performance with an employee, it can be easy just to focus on what is missing or incomplete, asking questions such as "What's the problem here?" or "Why are you still missing this goal?". That can be very demotivating, and whilst you cannot afford to let poor performance go unchallenged, there are more effective ways to focus on it. That's where coaching comes in!

Coaching enables you to help your people work out ways to achieve their personal performance goals and to come up with their own solutions to the challenges presented.

In order not to get bogged down in the detail, it helps to have a structure to work through when discussing how a team member can work to achieve their goals.

John Whitmore wrote a book called "Coaching for Performance" and this is used by coaches all over the world to help them structure a good coaching dialogue aimed at sustaining high performance. In his book, Whitmore introduces the 'GROW' model, giving coaches a logical flow to their discussions. GROW stands for Goal, Reality, Options, and Will. Asking questions in this sequence will help your people think about their goal in a logical way, shaping and structuring their own thought process to come up with ideas on how to achieve them.

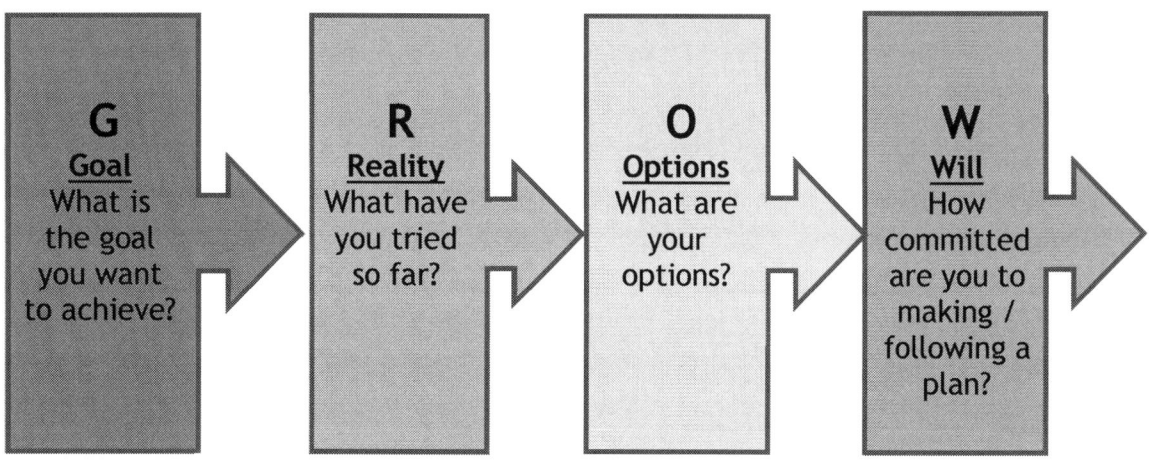

Manager as Coach

Coaching is a great way to help an employee to come up with their own solutions to a problem, and people are much more committed to seeing their own ideas succeed. Besides, if members of your team learn not to think for themselves, but always to defer to you, how will you ever find time for all the other elements of your role?

There are many well qualified and very experienced business coaches offering their services. Perhaps you have worked with one already. The good news is that you don't need to be a qualified coach in order to use a coaching style of management.

On the following page, there is a list of helpful coaching questions which you can use to get started. With time and practice, you will develop other questions for each stage that would help build focus and drive. In the meantime, you can simply use this list to get going.

If you want to GROW your people,

you can see why SPACE is so important!!

Bank of Coaching Questions

Goal
What exactly do you want to achieve?
Is it positive, desirable and challenging?
If you could have it, would you truly want it?
How measurable is it?
How will you know when you've achieved it?
By when do you want to complete it?
To what extent is it within your control?

Reality
What have you achieved so far in reaching this goal?
What have you learnt from that?
Could you break it down into more manageable sub-goals?
Who else do you need to help you reach your goal?
Who else will be affected if you achieve it?
Who do you know that has already succeeded in achieving this goal?
What external constraints are there to you achieving your goal (time, money etc)?
How might you constrain yourself (e.g., motivation, negative thinking etc)?
How might you overcome these obstacles?
What is *really* stopping you?
What might you be doing to sabotage your own efforts to reach this goal?

Options
What could you do as the next step towards reaching your goal?
What else could you do? And what else then?
If time / money / resources / people were not a factor, what could you do?
What would happen if you did nothing?
Who do you admire who already does this well?
What could you do that they do?

Will / Way Forward
Which options appeal most?
How will those options help you in achieving your goal?
Who else needs to know about your goal?
How and when will you inform them?
What obstacles do you expect to meet, and how will you overcome them?
What other priorities do you have that might divert your energy and motivation?
What will you do first?
How will you feel when you've succeeded?
How committed are you to moving forward with this (on a scale of 1-10)?
What would need to happen for your score to be higher?

Activity 5.3: My Goal – My Answers

Pick out a selection of questions on the previous page under each of the G-R-O-W headings, and use them to progress your own thinking and ideas about the goal you identified earlier. Write down your answers, here.

Did you manage to progress your thinking?

What could you try next time to make it even more effective?

Now try polishing your coaching skills by practising on a colleague.

Activity 5.4: Coaching Practice

The best way to test this process and to commit it to memory is to put some of the ideas into practice! Using the SMART goal you have written for yourself in activity 2.2, work with a friend or colleague to coach you on how to achieve it.

Take it in turn to play each of the following roles:

1. The coaching manager
2. The employee being coached

Use the forms on the following pages to note down your thoughts, ideas, feelings and feedback. Take as long as you need... don't rush it! Make a note so that you don't forget:

Round #1:

Coaching manager name:
Employee being coached name:
Observations:

Round #2:

Coaching manager name:
Employee being coached name:
Observations:

Round #3:

Coaching manager name:
Employee being coached name:
Observations:

Coaching Practice: COACHING MANAGER

How well did I prepare for this discussion?

What frame of mind was I in as we started?

Did my feelings change over the course of the discussion?

Did I manage to stay out of 'solutions' mode?

Did I help the other person to come to their own solution?

Did I test for commitment to the goal / course of action?

Which part of this activity am I most pleased about?

Which element would I definitely do differently next time?

How will I remember to integrate my experience and the feedback I received here into my coaching practice?

Coaching to Improve Performance

Understanding personal blockers, organisational interference and individual motivation is key to helping your people get out of their own way! Sometimes, despite best intentions, we manage to trip ourselves up on our journey to peak performance. That's precisely when some good coaching questions can really help.

If someone is falling short of their agreed performance, it can be helpful to consider the KASH model to diagnose where the root of the problem might be:

Knowledge:

- What is it that you are trying to achieve here?
- What is the positive difference it will make?
- Do you know how to achieve it?
- Who else do you know who has already achieved this?
- Could you ask them how they did it?

Attitude:
- How do you feel about trying to achieve this?
- Do you believe you can achieve it?
- Is your current mindset helping or hindering your progress?
- What are the consequences if you don't manage to do it?

Skills:
- Do you believe that you have the skills to do the task?
- What have you tried already, that has worked?
- What else do you need to learn to help you with this task right now?
- Who else has these skills and might be able to advise you?

Habit:
- Have you tried doing this in the past?
- How many times have you completed it successfully?
- If previous attempts haven't been successful, what else could you try?
- Practice makes perfect! How many times do you need to do this successfully before you know you've cracked it?

Directive Coaching

People have a tendency to complain about things that they could change, but have chosen not to, so they complain to vent their frustration at their own inertia. Just occasionally, some people may get stuck in their thinking about how to tackle a certain issue or complete a specific task, or convince themselves that they'll never be able to resolve it. As a result, you may find yourself coaching a colleague repeatedly on an issue you have already discussed.

That is a waste of your valuable time!

Not only is this a poor use of your time, but it is allowing them to avoid getting started. It may be that they are afraid of failing, or perhaps haven't understood exactly what is required. But sometimes, an individual may secretly be hoping that if they complain enough about it, you will take the problem away and deal with it yourself. Remember the tale of the spider in the bath? Well, fixing the problem for them is like moving the spider out of the bath. The problem gets solved this time, but they don't learn, and you have just added another task to your own to-do list.

Here's what to do instead:

First, you summarise your understanding of their issue:

"Ah yes, we've discussed this before, haven't we? Now, as I recall, the key elements are X, Y and Z."

Then, you remind them of what they had agreed to do:

"And if I remember rightly, you said you would do A, then B, and finally, C.   Have you started on A yet?"

Watch quietly as they shuffle uncomfortably, mumbling excuses, then...

"Right, so go and get started on A right away, please, and let me know how you get on."

Then go back to whatever you were doing, to signify that the conversation is closed, and the onus is now back firmly on them to start taking action.

Remember, the ideas, actions and strategies must be theirs, NOT YOURS, or it creates dependency on you, and they won't own it.

Ensure Success through High Commitment

You know you're doing a great job coaching when you help your people to identify their own solutions with a high level of commitment.

You have been discussing the goals and targets for each person in your team, and using coaching to get them to explore how they could achieve those goals. Once you have come up with an action plan, you need to test how committed they are to achieving it. One way of checking is to ask the person to rate their own level of commitment:

"So, on a scale of 1 – 10 (where 10 is 100% committed to achieving this), how committed are you?"

An answer of 1 – 4: Oh dear! Time to go back to the start, and make sure they understand why you are asking them to focus on this particular goal.

- "That seems very low. Tell me what's on your mind?"
- "Oh dear, seems as though you anticipate problems. Let's discuss those now."
- "That's a low score. Tell me about your other priorities."

An answer to 5 – 7: not bad, but still leaves a lot of wriggle-room! Ask more coaching questions to find out what would help their score to be higher:

- "How could we get that score higher, do you think? "
- "What would need to happen for that score to 10 out of 10, instead of only 6?"
- "What could get in the way of your success? And what do you want to do about that? How do you want to overcome that obstacle?"

An answer of 8 – 10: great! Is there still room for improvement with an 8 or 9?

- "Excellent news! Is there anything else you need from me in order for that to be 10/10?"
- "What will be your first step?"
- If 10/10: "Great! Let's catch up next month to see how you're getting on."

Tip:

When working on a behaviour or performance that needs improvement, remember to ask the team member to confirm their plan of action IN WRITING precisely what you have agreed they should work on. That helps to demonstrate that they have really understood. Also, when it's written by them, in their language, and emailed to you from their email account, it will be MUCH harder for them to claim they didn't know what they were supposed to be doing!

FAQ: What if they genuinely don't know the answer?

Sometimes people have good ideas, but lack the courage to voice them, in case they're wrong. Asking questions like "But what if you DID know?" or "If you were in my position, what do you think the answer would be?" or "What would a close friend advise you to do right now?" or "As the role expert, I know you will have some brilliant ideas on how to resolve this. Let's start by exploring some of those."

If that doesn't help to steer the conversation towards a solution, then (and only then) can you offer some suggestions of your own. But still go through the coaching questions to help the other person see how a possible solution might work in practice, and don't forget to check for commitment.

Chapter 5 personal reflections and insights

Take a moment now to reflect on what you have read in this chapter, and the exercises and activities you have completed. Be sure to extract the wisdom from your own insights, and apply it to improve your daily management practice.

- As a result of reading this chapter, I know how to use coaching to drive high performance, specifically, by...

- The main reasons for not jumping into 'solutions' mode, are:

- I will use the commitment scale to ensure that my team member is:

- I will always ensure that an employee confirms in writing their action plan, because:

Chapter Six: Sustaining High Performance

Reprioritisation in a busy world

Workloads are increasingly intense these days, and with competing priorities, it can be tricky to stay focused on what's most important. Eisenhower (34th president of the USA) devised a tool for prioritising his many tasks which transformed his personal effectiveness, and his approach is now used by some of the highest performing organisations and most successful professionals. The best way to make sure that you are working on the right things is to use the urgent and importance grid, as shown below:

Unfortunately, many people are so busy at work doing 'firefighting', that they never take time out to plan. If they did, they wouldn't spend so much time doing urgent but trivial tasks, and would spend more time doing important work.

No matter how crazy-busy you are at work, you're never Eisenhower-busy!

This is how <u>average managers</u> divide their time:

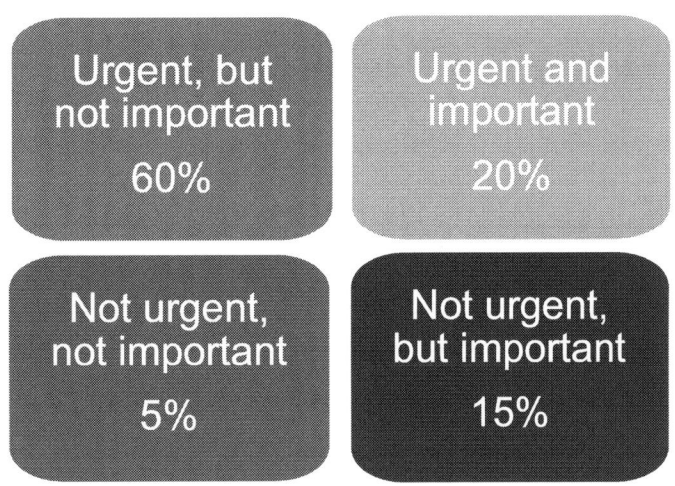

And THIS is how <u>high-performance managers</u> divide their time:

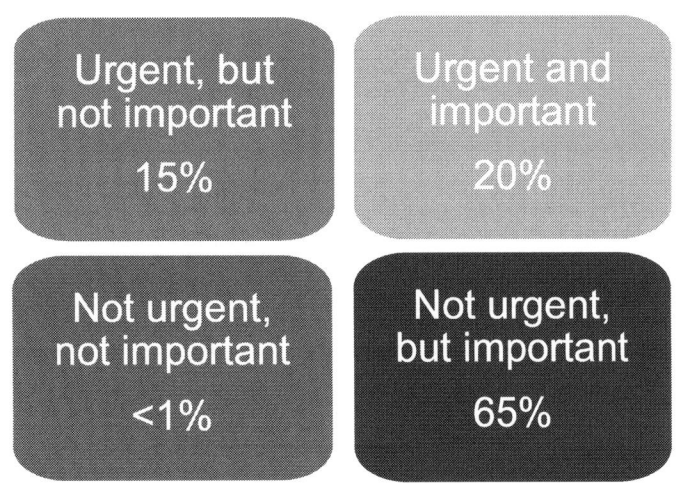

What a big difference you could make with some smart prioritisation!

Activity 6.1: Prioritising the Workload

Take a few moments to think about all the tasks you are required to complete over the course of a month. Which task belongs in which box?

#1: URGENT & IMPORTANT

-
-
-
-
-

#2: NOT URGENT, BUT IMPORTANT

-
-
-
-
-

#3: URGENT BUT NOT IMPORTANT

-
-
-
-
-

#4: NOT URGENT, NOT IMPORTANT

-
-
-
-
-

Write it down!

It is not enough simply to THINK about the tasks in priority order - you must write them down, otherwise you may forget important activities. You can write it on a piece of paper, on a flip chart or a white board next to your desk. Wherever you write it, put it somewhere very visible so that you can check your list on a daily basis, and reprioritise each morning, depending on the evolving needs of the business. Also, it will serve as a good example to your team.

Tip:

When someone comes to you and asks you to complete an urgent task for them, you can show them your prioritisation matrix, and tell them where it fits with your current list, and the time you have available. If the list is only in your head, it may appear that you are making excuses and not being helpful.

If you put the name or initials of the person for whom you are doing each task on your list, it can help to stop people queue-jumping. If somebody comes rushing into your office demanding you do an urgent task for them, you can refer them to your prioritisation matrix. Not only can they see that you already have a full workload for the day, but they can also see who you are working for. If they are more senior than the other names on your list, they have a right to ask you to do their task first. If they are less senior than the names on your list, they will be more likely to go and ask someone else instead.

- How can you use this to make sure you are putting the most important work at the very top of your to-do list?

- And how can you use this to help your people focus on the most important things every single day?!

Ownership & Accountability

High performance culture can only be achieved where employees have a strong sense of personal accountability. A blame culture, excuses, avoidance and back-stabbing are symptoms of a highly toxic culture.

The most successful people are those with really high levels of personal accountability, who do not blame others for their choices.

Mindset is a matter of choice. We can choose to feel like the victim in a challenging situation, or we can take ownership for the part we contributed to it.

When people are stuck in the Victim mindset, they say things like...
- It wasn't my fault!
- The guy never got back to me
- I was too busy
- Someone else let me down
- I don't remember agreeing to that

When people have high personal accountability, they say things like...
- I said I would do it, so even though it wasn't my responsibility, I did it.
- The guy didn't get back to me, so I went and found out who else could help
- I was very busy, but I prioritised it because I knew it was important
- That person let me down, so I spoke to someone else to resolve it
- It took some digging, but finally I found it.
- Entirely my fault, I completely forgot. I'm very sorry, I will fix that now.

What is the language you are hearing from the employees in your team?

One of the most effective things you can do when someone is blaming others for a task that they should have completed themselves, is to state what you hear:

"It sounds like you are blaming someone else for a task that was yours to complete. If I had paid you £1M bonus (or 'if your life depended on it') **to get this task completed properly, what would you have done differently to ensure it was done?"**

If the other person could have ensured task completion for £1M, then it absolutely is within their capability to resolve.

Some people find excuses, while others find a way.

Routes to Learning

Whenever we talk about learning and development, many people automatically think of formal training courses, but there are many ways to learn and develop, and taught courses form only a small part of this. Learning at work can be achieved by:

70%   'Experience' - On the job learning

20%   'Exposure' - Guidance from someone else

10%   'Education' – Attending formal training courses

Below, there are some ideas of how you can direct the people in your teams to the various sources of learning and development available.

70% Experience	20% Exposure	10% Education
• On the job experience • Job shadowing • Reading the process or the manual • New projects • Teaching others • Observation • Self learning • Reading • Researching best practice • e-Learning • Mentoring someone else on how to do it • Others?	• Working with more experienced people • Job shadowing • Working with a coach • Working with a mentor • Asking within your network • Implementing best practice approaches • Attending seminars • Conferences • Working groups • Reading a book or journal on the subject • TED talks and podcasts • Learning from someone else who has attended a course • Others?	• Attending a training course run internally or externally • Free online training programs, such as MOOC.org • Other online expert courses such as Udemy.com • Others?

As manager, don't forget to invest in your own development, too!

Personal Growth and Development

Helping your high performers to maintain their levels of success requires some careful thought.

Thinking back to the SPACE analysis, what is important to each person in your team, with particular regard to their aspirations? How could you help them to get closer to realising those aspirations?

Think specifically along the following lines:

- Role expansion
- High profile projects
- Additional training and development to support their career ambitions
- A mentor or coach
- Job shadowing
- Temporary secondment
- A lateral career move within the same company
- Time off to study or work towards a professional qualification
- Others?
-
-

FAQ: If they get too good, they'll be after my job

If the person in your team really is a high performer, they may have their eye on your job. Don't worry – there will be plenty of opportunity for you slowly to hand over some of your responsibilities, gradually delegating more and more, which will make your life easier in the long run. It will also free you up to make your next big move, too!

Other Team Development Ideas

Here are several other ideas to consider when thinking about growing and developing your team... and yourself! Some are better suited to certain types of organisation, and you will need to discuss some of them with HR before you get started.

- ## Book Club

If you don't have sufficient training budget for buying in training, consider doing a team book club. Allocate one professional text to each person on a subject which is personally and professionally relevant. Ask them to read it (give them a deadline), then to summarise the key learning points in a short presentation to the rest of the team. This is a great way to raise everyone's level of knowledge and share ideas about business improvement and best practice, for very little money.

- ## Cascade Training

Research shows that one of the best ways to embed new learning is to teach what you've learned to someone else. Sharing a synopsis of a training course attended is a fantastic way to get an even better return on the initial investment. A team member who is requesting formal training should agree in advance to deliver a cut-down version of that same training to the rest of the team. That way, you can quickly create a community of learning on the chosen topic.

- ## Open Training

If you are buying in a training course for your people, you could consider inviting people from other teams, or even other people from within your professional network on a reciprocal basis. It is reasonable to expect that if your company invites people from another company to attend your training, they should return the favour and offer people from your company the opportunity to attend training that they have arranged.

- ## Set up a Knowledge Network

This activity involves inviting people from across your professional network (in non-competing organisations) to meet up and discuss ideas and practices which have worked in their organisation which might also work in yours. You could invite members of your team to be speakers at these events, which will help to cement their learning, and raise their professional profile. This activity works well if you arrange it for every couple of months. There is no cost (except maybe for coffee and bacon rolls), but members have to be invited to join the network.

- ## Work Placements or Role Exchange

Again, look to your professional network, and see if there is another comparable (but non-competing) organisation with a great reputation and high performance culture. You could consider arranging a work placement exchange with a high performer in your team and a high performer in theirs. Each employee swaps roles and desks for a prescribed period (maybe 3 – 6 months) in order to gain experience in another organisation without running the risk of losing them to the competition. The cost for this is usually minimal – your team member stays on your payroll, and the employee from the organisation still gets paid by their employer. There is a huge opportunity to cross-pollinate learning, share ideas about best practice and collaborate on improvement projects together.

- ## Lunch & Learn

Create a programme of speakers on topics of interest to you and your team. These will typically be colleagues from other departments or parts of the organisation. They may be speaking on a change programme they have been involved in, or a business improvement idea they might have tried, or be an expert on a particular subject which could be really helpful to your own department. As part of this same approach, you might also suggest to members of your team to run a Lunch & Learn session of their own to share their education and experience to anyone who is interested. This is also a great way to share knowledge within the organisation.

- ## Coffee Mornings

Many managers complain that employees tend to think and work in silos, giving little consideration to how their work affects other departments. A great way around this is to run a series of coffee mornings, inviting employees from different parts of the business process to come over and join your team for doughnuts, and to talk about some of the challenges of working together, the dependencies, and what happens when either team doesn't get all the information they need. You could use the "good… even better if…" structure here to facilitate a positive conversation about better interdepartmental collaboration, and mapping the end to end business process, so that everyone can better understand the part they play.

Chapter 6 personal reflections and insights

Take a moment now to reflect on what you have read in this chapter, and the exercises and activities you have completed. Be sure to extract the wisdom from your own insights, and apply it to improve your daily management practice.

- As a result of reading this chapter, I know that using a prioritisation matrix will help me to:

- Using a prioritisation matrix will help my team to:

- Using a prioritisation matrix will reduce queue-jumping and overloading because:

- When people start making excuses for work they haven't done, I can gently remind them that:

- In order to help my team members to learn and grow, I will explore the following three development ideas:

Chapter Seven: Reward & Recognition

The best way to encourage good performance is to reward it every time it happens, until it becomes a habit.

This simple formula will help you to improve the performance and behaviour of every one of your team members.

Catch them doing something right! When someone has a great idea, supports a colleague, goes the extra mile by making additional effort, be sure to say thank you.

FAQ: Doesn't it raise their expectation of a pay rise?

Some managers worry that giving too much praise or positive feedback sets the expectation of a pay rise or a promotion which may not be forthcoming, so they tend to dumb down their attempts at recognition. As mentioned before, this can lead to a decline in performance and engagement and make for more work for the line manager in the long run.

Some managers take the view that if you say thank you, you risk encouraging complacency. But try <u>not</u> saying thank you, and run the risk of your employees believing that you take them for granted. The results will be much worse!

FAQ: I shouldn't need to keep saying well done. Still having a job should be all the reward they need.

Occasionally, a manager will say that they don't need to say thank you. The very fact that their employee still has a job should surely be thanks enough. However, high performing staff will be more likely to look for a job elsewhere if they think you haven't noticed their efforts. "You don't know how lucky you are" rarely convinces a demotivated employee.

Many people think of 'reward' as only being financial, and worry that they don't have the budget available to give a discretionary bonus or grant a pay rise. In truth, however, reward can take many forms. Chocolate, going home on time, training courses, flexible working arrangements... all of these can be used to reward good performance.

HOW people like to be recognised for good performance will depend on their personality type and their career and personal priorities. Check back to the SPACE analysis to reward them with something they will really appreciate.

Activity 7.1: How many other types of reward can you identify?

-
-
-
-
-
-
-

A person who feels appreciated will <u>always</u> do more than expected.

Activity 7.2: What does recognition mean to you?

What do YOU like to be recognised for?

How do you like to receive that recognition?

How do you feel when your efforts go unappreciated?

And how does that affect your performance?

Activity 7.3: Recognition Plan for Members of My Team

Now, go back to the list of people in your team, and identify at least one thing for which you would like to give some recognition and praise.

- **Person:**

Recognition:

- **Person:**

Recognition:

- **Person:**

Recognition:

- **Person:**

Recognition:

- **Person:**

Recognition:

- **Person:**

Recognition:

- **Person:**

Recognition:

- **Person:**

Recognition:

Chapter 7 personal reflections and insights

Take a moment now to reflect on what you have read in this chapter, and the exercises and activities you have completed. Be sure to extract the wisdom from your own insights, and apply it to improve your daily management practice.

- As a result of reading this chapter, I now understand that as well as financial rewards, I could also try:

- Not getting recognition for good work feels like:

- I will take the following steps to give specific praise and recognition to each person in my team:

Conclusion

If you have a poor performer in your team, and you aren't addressing it, there are actually two poor performers in your team. Ignoring under performance means that you are part of the problem, and will likely be on someone else's underperformance radar.

The way you manage the performance of people in your team will be what sets you apart as having leadership potential.

Good performance management can transform a stressful work environment into a team spirit which is energised, motivated and optimistic about the future.

Everybody will have to have some Crucible Conversations™ at some point in their career. You now have all the tools and techniques you need to prepare for and navigate those discussions with confidence.

FAQ: There may be some good ideas here in theory, but I'm too busy doing the day job for all this touchy-feely stuff!

The day-to-day operational work needs to be done by your team, allocated and coordinated by you. That's what management is all about. If you are too busy working on operational tasks, check back to the career trajectories graph on page 9. Are you sure you're really cut out to be a manager?

It may seem touchy-feely, but if you don't invest the time to focus on your people properly, you will spend a lot more time resolving conflict, reporting sickness and absence, managing under performance, dealing with disengagement, reading CVs and interviewing new people. And that will all reflect on your own credibility as a manager. So, get the people stuff sorted sooner rather than later, and you will find that you have a happier, more engaged and more productive team, and your career will really go from strength to strength, too.

Our people should be our greatest asset; they are usually our greatest operating expense, and we need to get the best out of that human asset. Follow these steps, and you will be well on your way to creating a high-performance team.

At a glance...

Here's a handy reminder of all the tools and techniques covered in this workbook and how to use them to greatest effect to drive high performance at work.

	Setting goals	Checking progress	Coaching for improvement	Managing under performance	Sustaining high performance
Work motivators	Y		Y	Y	Y
SPACE analysis	Y	Y	Y	Y	Y
Engagement questions	Y	Y	Y	Y	Y
Goal alignment	Y	Y	Y	Y	Y
SMART goals	Y	Y	Y	Y	Y
1:1 meetings		Y	Y	Y	Y
Unconscious bias	Y	Y	Y	Y	
Think, Feel, Do		Y	Y	Y	Y
Willing & Able		Y	Y	Y	
Honesty & respect		Y	Y	Y	
Crucible Conversations™			Y	Y	
GROW model	Y	Y	Y	Y	Y
Coaching questions	Y	Y	Y	Y	Y
KASH	Y	Y	Y	Y	Y
70:20:10	Y	Y	Y	Y	Y
Team development	Y				Y

Action Planning

In this workbook is a list of methodologies to help you manage performance effectively, and to build a high performing, engaged team. As you have worked your way through, you have completed a number of activities to understand yourself and to help you understand the individual members of your team as a way to unlocking high performance. Now it is time to pull together all those individual action plans into one integrated plan for each person who reports into you.

Learning about the process is only half the job, though. Now, you need to put it all into action. Nothing changes if you don't change it!

Go back through your answers to each of the activities you completed, and pull together a solid plan of action to help your team to raise their game.

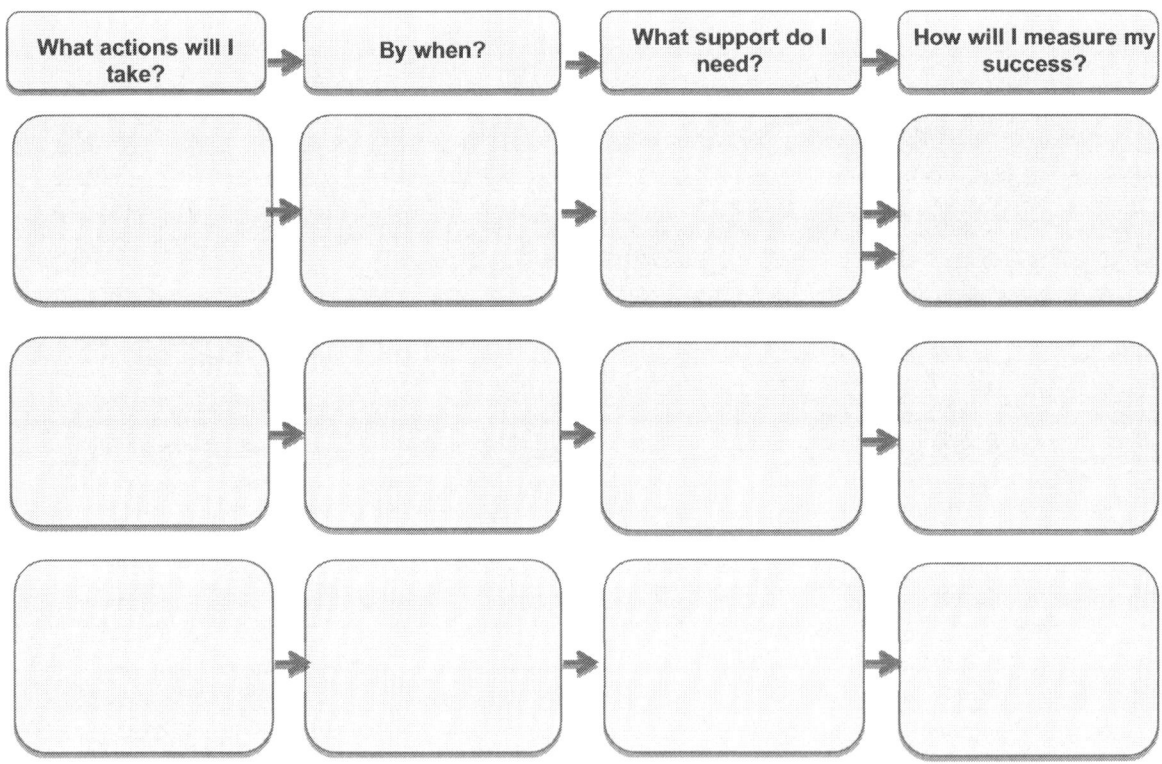

What actions will I take?	By when?	What support do I need?	How will I measure my success?

You get the people you deserve,
so, make sure you're the manager with the best people!

Further Reading

This workbook will get you off to a flying start, but to enhance your knowledge of managing people for high performance, you might like to read these books:

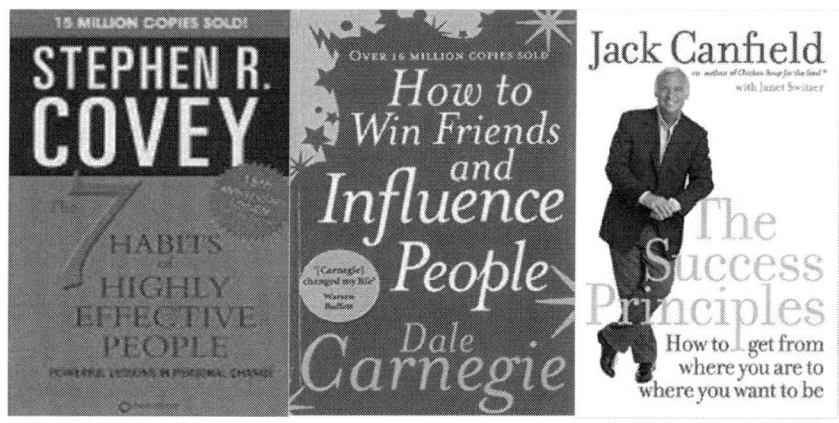

Check out their websites, too: there is a wealth of additional material from these leading thinkers.

Notes:

Notes:

Printed in Great Britain
by Amazon

16852474R00061